Seaplanes

HANS HALBERSTADT

Seaplanes

HANS HALBERSTADT

MetroBooks

MetroBooks

An Imprint of Friedman/Fairfax Publishers

Library of Congress Cataloging-in-Publication Data

Halberstadt, Hans.
    Seaplanes / Hans Halberstadt.
        p.   cm.
    Includes bibliographical references and index
    ISBN 1-56799-879-8
    1. Seaplanes—History.   I. Title.
TL684.H35   1999   99-36732
629.133'347—dc21   CIP

Editor: Ann Kirby
Art Director: Kevin Ullrich
Designer: Jennifer O'Connor
Photography Editor: Amy Talluto
Production Manager: Richela Fabian

Color separations by Bright Arts Graphics (S) Pte. Ltd.
Printed in Hong Kong by Sing Cheong Printing Company Ltd.
1 3 5 7 9 10 8 6 4 2

For bulk purchases and special sales, please contact:
Friedman/Fairfax Publishers
Attention: Sales Department
15 West 26th Street
New York, NY 10010
212/685-6610 FAX 212/685-1307

Visit our website:
www.metrobooks.com

Contents

Preface

Once upon a time, very long ago, I had the good fortune to be a kid who lived near a seaplane base. Our home was on a hill overlooking Richardson's Bay, a quiet estuary about ten miles (16km) north of San Francisco's Golden Gate Bridge. There, just a mile away, were a couple of small hangars, a ramp, and a motley assortment of amphibious creatures of the air.

The place was called Commodore Aviation, and their stock in trade was sight-seeing rides for the most adventurous tourists visiting San Francisco. For ten dollars you could get a quick peek at the famous city from overhead, and Commodore's little aircraft seemed to be doing a booming business. I watched them taxi out to the center of the little bay, turn into the wind, accelerate, and lift gracefully into the air. In a few minutes, they were back, gliding gracefully back down to the water.

I was captivated by aviation in general and by these little planes in particular. A paper route provided the necessary cash, and one bright day I hiked down the hill, down the railroad tracks, to take my first airplane ride.

Three tourists and I were ushered to a Republic Seabee and installed in our seats. The pilot climbed aboard and fired up. He taxied out into the bay, turned into the wind, and pushed the throttle forward. The Seabee roared ahead and quickly was up on the step, spray flying left and right. In a moment we were up. We turned, gained altitude, and I saw the world in a new way—from the air, for the first time.

The flight was very brief, probably no more than fifteen minutes. We cruised past the Golden Gate, over San Francisco, then back north again. All too soon we glided back down to Richardson's Bay, taxied back to the ramp, and were again on solid ground.

But that flight changed my life. Only a few years later I started sky-diving, and almost immediately, at age eighteen, I went to war in aircraft, this time in helicopters. I've been involved in aviation one way or another for most of the forty years since that first flight. I've flown little planes and big ones, but the most memorable of all was that Seabee, long ago.

It has been some time, but that seaplane business is still in operation, right there on Richardson's Bay. They still take tourists up for a quick look at the upper side of San Francisco, and an aerial tour of the Golden Gate Bridge and Alcatraz and the bay. It costs more than ten dollars now, but it is still affordable for a kid with a paper route. And kids with paper routes are still discovering the delights of aviation with their first rides in a seaplane.

One of the most versatile seaplane designs, the Republic Seabee made flying fun. Here, a Seabee comes in for a smooth landing on the Alaskan waterfront.

Acknowledgments

Writing a book is sometimes a lot less work than you might think. When the topic is near and dear, it is a labor of love, and over too soon. And when the object of your affections is beloved by others, sometimes you all share. That's the way it was with this one; the little fraternity of aviation writers to which I belong is a generous crew, and I had no trouble getting other people to do a lot of my work.

As usual, Mike Green, legendary author of books about military subjects, once again lent me most of the references needed for this work, plus supplied lots of great contacts and a pile of wonderful photographs. Tom Murphy, who would have been able to write this thing with his eyes closed, shared even more useful material, and more contacts.

Many veteran seaplane pilots from World War II, the Korean War era, and since graciously shared stories, recollections, and contacts. Among them were Howard Bowman, a veteran of many missions in flying boats; Capt. J. D. Mooney, U.S.N (Ret), a career Navy officer who started flying Catalinas in 1941, and who shared his memories and expertise and some great war stories; and Rod Bittencurt, a Mars crewman from the 1950s, who contributed the most interesting kind of history of all—personal reminiscences and recollections from missions across the Pacific.

Canadian bush pilots are notoriously interesting characters, and Kaviv Momoh certainly fits the mold. His account of floatplane operations in the backwoods of Ontario is delightful.

I am indebted also to Steven Price and Charlie at San Francisco Seaplane Tours for the instruction in the Beaver.

Disclaimer

One of the challenges of any kind of historical study involves sorting out conflicting claims about who did what to whom. Books on aviation history are notorious examples. Reference works sometimes conflict badly on just when a first flight occurred, when a new design entered service, or exactly when a particular aircraft first used Pratt and Whitney R-1830 radial engines. I have been forced to select the most apparently reliable data, so discerning readers may find conflicts here with data printed elsewhere. Without a time machine to go back and observe the actual events, such conflicts are inevitable.

![biplane]

CHAPTER 1

Pioneers of Sky and Sea

Flying Boats from Langley to the First World War

According to gospel, the age of flight began with the Wright brothers' famous flight at Kitty Hawk, North Carolina, in December of 1903. But long before Wilbur and Orville made that epic flight, other men were building aircraft and trying to get them to work. Some of these were designed to operate from water rather than from land, and a floatplane came close to beating the Wrights for the honor of the first powered heavier-than-air flight.

Students of aviation history still debate the merits of Professor Samuel Pierpont Langley (1834–1906) and his experimental 1903 floatplane. While the Wrights were busy at Kitty Hawk, Langley was busy preparing a competitor. Sponsored by the Smithsonian Institution and the U.S. government to the tune of $70,000, Langley's plane—called the Aerodrome—was well designed and constructed. It was apparently an airworthy design that should have worked, but a premature launch from its catapult—before its engine was run up to full power— destroyed the fledgling seaplane. Langley didn't attempt to rebuild it (he died a few years later), and the accident produced a lot of negative publicity about powered flight.

13

This wonderful photograph shows a Benoist seaplane about 300 feet (91m) in the air.

14

Langley's 1903 Aerodrome, modified by Glenn Curtiss, takes to the air, Curtiss himself bravely at the helm. In the rush to create the first successful heavier-than-air flying machine, this floatplane came close to beating out the Wright brothers. Right: A Short S-38 is hoisted aboard HMS Africa shortly before Commander Sampson's 1912 demonstration takeoff.

After the failures of Langley and other early flight experimenters, the Wright brothers' success at Kitty Hawk was met with much skepticism by the press and the scientific community. In fact, a complete written account of their achievement did not appear in print until March 1904. It wasn't until about 1905 that the idea of flying machines really took off, and then it did so with a bang.

Innovators suddenly cropped up all over the place, building their own versions of the Wrights' flying machine, tweaking the designs as they went along. Racing airplanes became a very popular and media-hyped sport, and early pilots became celebrities along the lines of modern-day athletes.

Taking to the Water

Some early innovators turned their sights back toward the sea, where Langley had placed his dreams of flight back in 1903. Operating from water had some obvious advantages—as well as disadvantages—for these early fliers. The surface of lakes and bays offered smooth, long, and perfectly level areas for landings and takeoffs. If you crashed in one of these early flying machines, water might make for a softer landing. But operating from water demanded floatation gear of some kind, and that added weight and drag. The tiny 20- and 30-horsepower (hp) engines available before 1910 had enough trouble with the weight and drag of the flimsy land machines and their negligible landing gear.

The first successful floatplane didn't take off until 1910, with Frenchman Henri Fabre at the helm. Fabre made his first flight in March of that year, and kept at it until September. His little contraption could stay aloft for two miles (3.2km) by then—at which point, M. Fabre retired from the business, his hide and honor intact, and was never heard from again.

But many more innovators followed. As aviation grew, the desire to take off and land on water grew with it.

Fast Forward: The Seaplane Takes Off

In the years before World War I, many kinds of float designs and hull designs were tried, all over Europe and the United States. Some were more boatlike than others, and some began to integrate the hull with the airframe of the aircraft, enclosing, in many examples, the fuselage entirely. The wings and tail still looked like a box kite on steroids, but the trend during this time toward lower drag and better stability was rapid.

Some manufacturers, such as Short in Britain, committed to twin-float designs, while American inventor Glenn Curtiss and others developed the single-float and "flying boat" approach. Curtiss built the first successful seaplane in 1911. The first twin-float seaplane appeared in 1912, designed by Commander Schwann of the Royal Navy, a little Avro powered by an inadequate 35-hp engine. The first monoplane on floats appeared that same year, a Borel with an 80-hp power plant; this design served the Royal Navy as a trainer for several years. A large, powerful, and innovative Italian monoplane, the Guidoni, successfully dropped a 700-pound (320kg) torpedo during a demonstration in 1914.

The U.S. Navy started working with catapults in 1912. The first trial, with a

In the early days, catapults were used to launch seaplanes into the air. Here, a Curtiss N-9 training plane awaits such a takeoff in March 1918.

A Curtiss flying boat skims low over the sea.

18

Glenn Curtiss, on the left, shows off his flying boat.

Curtiss E, destroyed the aircraft. Even so, the technique held promise and further tests and modifications were tried. Another trial, on November 12, 1912, successfully launched a Curtiss Navy A-3, and other trials followed. A catapult was installed on the U.S.S. *North Carolina*, and a Curtiss F made, in 1916, the first successful "cat shot" from a warship in U.S. Navy history.

Also about this time, more efficient hull and float designs were invented. Instead of the scow-shaped, flat-bottomed floats used until this time, seaplanes began to be designed with V-shaped hulls with a pronounced "step" or notch toward the rear. As an aircraft with these modifications accelerated during takeoff, the float lifted up out of the water, reducing the surface area in contact

with the water and reducing drag. The step was discovered to break the suction under the hull or float, making it much easier for the pilot to get the airplane "unstuck."

Curtiss's Flying Boat

In the United States, Glenn Curtiss had been experimenting with floatplanes since 1908. These experiments finally paid off in January

You'd look grim, too, if you were supposed to get this thing airborne. It's another of Glenn Curtiss's designs, a 1913 monoplane version of the flying boat.

1911 with a float-equipped Curtiss Model D and a flight from the calm surface of San Diego Bay near North Island.

Curtiss was a true aviation pioneer. In addition to his historic flights, including the first public flight of more than one kilometer in July 1909, he was responsible for many key advances in aviation design. Perhaps his most important invention was the aileron, which provided lateral control of the wings of the aircraft, something the Wrights and others had struggled with. Curtiss, an early competitor of the Wright brothers, would attempt to invalidate their patents in 1914 by proving that Langley's Aerodrome (which predated the Wrights' machine) was indeed capable of flight.

Other of Curtiss's great innovations were specific to seaplanes. In May 1911,

while operating from Lake Keuka, New York, the float on Curtiss's Model D was damaged during a takeoff and some water leaked aboard. The volume of water wasn't enough to keep the aircraft from taking off, so Curtiss was airborne before he noticed a problem. When he pushed his control wheel forward to return to the surface, those few gallons of water sloshed to the front of the pontoon, shifting the center of gravity far forward. He couldn't control the plane, and it crashed into the lake. Over land, such an event would have been promptly fatal, but Curtiss emerged from the water unscathed and with his enthusiasm for aviation undampened. From then on, all floats had watertight internal bulkheads to prevent such accidents.

Shortly after this incident Curtiss built a modified floatplane with the pilot's position inside the float. After years of disinterest, the U.S. military began around this time to take a serious interest in aviation. Curtiss supplied the Navy's first floatplane in 1911, the A-1, and another, the A-2 OWL (for "Over Water or Land"), both with retractable wheels as well as floats. Small floats on each wingtip provided stability. By the next year, 1912, the U.S. Navy was testing a rather advanced-looking Curtiss Model E "Flying Fish." While underpowered, the Flying Fish was the first practical flying boat, a design concept Curtiss immediately patented.

The Short Brothers

In England, the Short brothers began experimenting in 1907 with gliders and with powered aircraft a year later. Their first off-spring was powered with a 40-hp automobile engine that was too heavy to get off the ground. By 1909 the Short Brothers were building airplanes for the Wright brothers under license, providing experience and

building a reputation. It was the foundation of a company that would become one of the international giants of aviation and the British leader of seaplane and flying boat design in the 1930s and '40s.

Col. Mervyn O'Gorman took over the British Army Aircraft Factory in 1911 and promptly started developing powered, manned aircraft for the military. The British Army and Navy soon started to assume responsibility for the integration of airplanes into their battle plans, a development that inspired enthusiasts like the Shorts and other aviation pioneers of the time, all of whom began working on military designs. Army Aircraft Trials were held during August 1912; over thirty manufacturers participated.

The Shorts' first seaplane took to the air in April 1912, a substantial machine with enclosed fuselage, 100-hp Gnome engine, accommodations for pilot and passenger, and enough fuel to stay aloft for six hours. The floats were made of plywood and balloon fabric, with wingtip and tail floats made of inflated rubberized fabric. After a test flight, it was consigned to the care and custody of a then Lt. Sampson, Royal Navy. Sampson took it to the big Weymouth Naval Review in May, and then set a record with it in 1912, with a flight of 195 miles (312km) in 194 minutes. Sixty miles per hour (96kph) was a respectable speed at the time, but not for long.

During the Fleet Review of 1912, another Short airplane became the first to be launched from a moving ship, HMS *Hibernia*, traveling at 10½ knots. By this time, the Admiralty was buying airplanes of all shapes and abilities, from many manufacturers, and naval officers were finally thinking seriously about how they might be employed.

While others concentrated on land planes during this prewar era, the Shorts

21

Launching the first Boeing on Lake Union, Seattle, 1916.

A Short S310 Type-A torpedo assault plane, ready for action. Note the rather large torpedo suspended between the floats.

abandoned the Wright style of design and began to specialize primarily in seaplanes. They developed a twin-engine aircraft, too, and taught many British naval officers to fly—all of which was excellent preparation for the busy times to come.

The Shorts' biggest success of World War I was its Admiralty Type 184, ordered by the Royal Naval Air Service first in 1914. This two-seat seaplane used a 225-hp Sunbeam engine, and was affectionately known by its crews as the "225." Another highly successful model was the Short Seaplane Model 827, which featured a 150-hp Sunbeam engine and a fully enclosed fuselage. This floatplane had a wingspan of nearly 54 feet (16.5m), a top speed of 61 mph (98kph), and could stay aloft for 3½ hours. Armed with a Lewis gun and bombs, the Short 827 was a valuable machine, modern for its day, and served throughout the First World War.

Boeing's B&W and Model C

While the European powers were slaughtering each other in the mud of France and the Low Countries, American aviation was watching closely and learning some lessons. Out in Washington state, William Boeing became interested in aviation after building a fortune in the timber industry. He learned to fly in 1915 and bought a Martin trainer soon after. The trainer became a model for an improved 1916 aircraft—a floatplane named the B&W, built with George Westervelt—the ancestor of all the great Boeing designs.

The B&W operated easily from the generally placid waters around Seattle. It was designed to be a utility seaplane, with a wingspan of 52 feet (16m), a gross weight of 2,800 pounds (1,270kg), and a 125-hp Hall-Scott A-5 engine. It was a conventional machine with a bit of extra power and a few other enhancements. Top speed was 67 mph (107kph) and maximum range 320 miles

(512km). Boeing and Westervelt offered the plane to the U.S. Navy, which politely declined. New Zealand bought a few, where they delivered mail and set an altitude record for that nation, at 6,500 feet (1,980m).

At the same time, though, Bill Boeing was working on another design of his own, a side-by-side trainer slightly smaller than the B&W, with a smaller 100-hp engine but a bit better top speed, 72.7 mph (116kph). This aircraft, the Model C, flew just four months after the first flight of the B&W, in November 1916. Sales of fifty-three Model Cs to the U.S. Navy followed, and the U.S. Army bought three with wheels only.

Launching into World War I

By 1914, with tensions between the major and minor European powers rapidly rising, seaplanes were serious business. By the time hostilities broke out in August 1914, quite a few designs were either in service with the competing powers, or were close to acceptance. Stopwith had launched the Bat Boat in 1913, an airplane with a sharp, speedboat-shaped hull and tail surfaces supported by booms rather than the conventional fuselage.

Curtiss designed a large flying boat, the H-1, to compete for the record for the first transatlantic flight. The basic design was quickly adopted by the Royal Navy (with modifications), and christened the H-4. Curtiss seaplanes were normally operated from calm San Diego Bay or protected lakes and inlets; British military aircraft would have to operate from the rough waters of the English Channel and surrounding waters.

During acceptance tests, Lt. J. C. Porte had to fight the aircraft during taxi and landing operations. He proposed a modification program for the Curtiss H-4s that extended and sharpened the V of the hull, and changed the shape and placement of the steps. The revised aircraft, known as the Felixstowe F1, inspired a

larger design, the F2, with twin 325-hp Rolls-Royce engines, a 95-foot 7½-inch (29m) wingspan, and a maximum speed of about 90 mph (144kph). They and their wartime descendants had excellent endurance and were well suited to patrol missions, but they were lightly armed and vulnerable to enemy fighters. Even so, one of them downed a German airship over England. By the time the war concluded in November 1918, the basic concept had been scaled up to the F5L, with 103-foot (31.5m) wingspans, 400-hp American Liberty engines, mission endurance time of eight hours, and a 920-pound (418kg) payload of bombs. More than three hundred of the F5s were built in Britain and the United States.

Germany, Italy, and France all put many excellent flying boats and floatplanes in service during the war. Among the most advanced was Dornier's big Rs I, a huge, sleek, all-metal biplane. Powered by three Maybach 240-hp engines, it was a remarkable design for 1914, and was superior to many later flying boats. It would be many years before some manufacturers appreciated the virtues of metal fabrication for hull and empennage construction.

The Austro-Hungarian Navy used an excellent single-engine flying boat, the Lohner Type L. This slender machine was very successful for its time and its mission. Although powered with only a single 160-hp Austro-Daimler engine, the Lohner L could get up to 105 mph (168kph), carry a 441-pound (200kg) bomb load, and provided cold, breezy accommodations for a crew of two.

23

CHAPTER 2

Marine Aviation Comes of Age

Developments of the Twenties and Thirties

In the very few years since the Wright brothers' first flight, aviation had made tremendous advances. The first aircraft were slow, fragile, greatly underpowered, extremely dangerous, and highly experimental. Real development had only begun around 1910, but a combination of public enthusiasm and the pressures of war quickly produced tangible results: by around 1916, aircraft were becoming useful, practical, moderately reliable devices. And while they were still underpowered, new engine technologies were gradually improving performance. By the 1920s, seaplane designs of all sizes and shapes were roaring into the air all over the world.

Across the Atlantic: The Navy-Curtiss

In 1917 the U.S. Navy awarded a contract to Glenn Curtiss for a very good (for the time) long-range patrol aircraft, the NC (for Navy-Curtiss). As originally conceived, the NC flying boats would provide cover for convoys and naval forces operating between America and Europe, finding and attacking German submarines and surface combatants.

25

To shorten mail delivery between Germany and the United States, the Norddeutscher Lloyd's ship Bremen was fitted with a catapult, which launched this He 12 seaplane from up to 500 miles (800km) at sea.

It was one of those things that seemed like a good idea at the time—the Olmstead propeller installed on a Curtiss 109 floatplane, October 1917.

It was a clean, capable design—a 45-foot (13.5m) hull of advanced form, three big Liberty engines of 400-hp each, 126-foot (38.5m) wingspan, and almost 70 feet (21m) long. Empty, the NC weighed 16,000 pounds (7,300kg); fuel, crew, and weapons could add another 11,000 pounds (5,000kg).

By the time the NC was fully fledged, though, the war was virtually over. The first NC flew in October 1918, just weeks before the armistice was signed on November 11. The prototype flew again on November 25, this time stuffed to the gills with fifty-one extra passengers, a world record for the time. Even so, the Navy decided that three engines didn't provide enough power for the kinds of missions expected, and a fourth was added to the design.

In 1913 the British newspaper the *Daily Mail* offered a prize of £10,000 for the first nonstop flight across the Atlantic. World War I prevented any serious attempts at the competition, but the U.S. Navy decided they had a suitable aircraft, and attempted the feat—not for the money, but to demonstrate the Navy's capability in a new, technological world.

Four NCs were built, numbers 1 through 4. Originally, all four were to attempt the crossing in loose formation. NC-1, though, sustained some damage in a storm and the second aircraft, NC-2, was cannibalized to provide parts.

Commander John Towers, commanding officer and navigator for NC-3, had responsibility for the whole operation. The three NCs took off from Rockaway, New York, on May 8, 1919, en route to Trepassay, Newfoundland, the starting point for the epic attempt. Two hours out, NC-4's engines lost power; she landed at sea, then taxied in to Chatham, Massachusetts, where the Naval Air Station repaired the engines. NC-1 and NC-3 pressed on and landed at Halifax, Nova Scotia, after a long day in the air.

The next morning, as the pair prepared to press on, preflight inspections disclosed cracks in the propellers, so they were forced to stay put for a day of repairs. NC-4 was still at Chatham, far down the coast, prevented from continuing by high winds and a powerful storm.

The weather improved enough by May 14 for NC-4 to take up the chase, but Commander Towers didn't feel like waiting. The two flying boats taxied out, advanced their throttles—and couldn't get off the water. Both were overloaded with fuel. They taxied back and abandoned the attempt for that day.

NC-4 finally joined them, and on May 16, in much improved weather, all three aircraft blasted down the harbor. Just before dusk, the three staggered into the air, slowly gained altitude, and shaped course for the Azores, settling in for the long flight.

Below, at 50-mile (80km) intervals, were stationed U.S. Navy destroyers, in order to provide navigation assistance and rescue if required. All three aircraft flew independently, rather than in formation, partly because NC-4 was faster than the others, and partly because formation flying at night was—and is—demanding and dangerous, and the flight was perilous enough as it was.

Dawn found all three aircraft closing in on the Azores, safe and sound—for the moment. But with the dawn came fog and clouds. Fifteen hours out of Newfoundland, nearly successful, the flight was suddenly threatened with disaster. The fog was so thick at times that the crews could not see the tail surfaces of their own planes.

Low on fuel and disoriented, Commander Towers brought NC-1 down on the open ocean, intending to wait for the fog to clear enough to get a navigational sight on the sun with his sextant. He got his fix, but with seas running to 12 feet (3.5m) he could not get the aircraft airborne again.

Curtiss NC-4, typical of post–World War I flying boats operated by the U.S. Navy.

Meanwhile, NC-4 closed on the island chain, with Lt. Commander Albert Read navigating and serving as aircraft commander. Through the fog, the island of Flores appeared; Read could tell where he was, and pressed on. The fog closed in again, though, and when another island, Faial, momentarily appeared, Read ordered the plane down. They slid back to the water at the little town of Horta, shortly before noon. The U.S. Navy cruiser *Columbia*, one of the support ships for the flight, was waiting in the harbor.

NC-1 and her crew were still out on the open ocean, still unable to take off, and still surrounded by fog. The heavy seas beat on the unfortunate aircraft. It wasn't long before the crew's thoughts were of survival rather than on the success of the transatlantic flight. Fortunately, a Greek freighter, the *Ionia*, materialized out of the fog and sent over one of its boats to rescue the crew. NC-1 was abandoned to the sea, and sunk three days later.

Meanwhile at sea, Commander Towers and NC-3 were down on the surface, also suffering from the harsh conditions. After making a wrong turn and running low on fuel, Towers figured he was close to the Azores but didn't know exactly where they were. NC-3 landed hard in rough seas, collapsing the center struts and ending the flight. He put the aircraft into "boat" mode and waited for the fog to clear or for someone to rescue

Royal Air Force Schneider Cup team for 1931 with their Supermarine S6B aircraft.

them. It would have been a shorter wait if Towers had not left his radio transmitter back in Newfoundland in an effort to save weight. It took two days, but NC-3 finally drifted close to the island of São Miguel and Towers used the last of his fuel to taxi into the harbor of Ponta Delgada.

Only one of the original four aircraft was airworthy, Lt. Cdr. Read's NC-4, and now the sole survivor prepared to finish

the mission. They took off on May 20, flew to Ponta Delgada, landed, and then were caught again by the weather. It would be another week before they could take off again, but they got away at 0818 hours on May 27.

Below, another picket line of Navy destroyers marked the route, and one by one NC-4 passed them by overhead. Eleven and a half hours later, in evening twilight,

the crew of NC-4 spotted the flashing light of Cabo da Roca lighthouse on the coast of Spain. Read ordered a turn to the south, and half an hour later, about eight in the evening, NC-4 glided down to alight on the Tagus estuary at Lisbon. A major milestone in the development of flight had been achieved, just sixteen years after the first successful flight of the Wrights' machine at Kitty Hawk.

The Schneider Trophy Races

Like any other fad, aviation captured the attention of many promoters, honest and otherwise. As a spur to promote the development of airplanes generally and seaplanes specifically, in 1913 a French newspaper publisher established La Coupe D'Aviation Maritime Jacques Schneider, a race for seaplanes. Commonly known as the Schneider Cup, this competition did not at first attract a lot of attention, but in the years following World War I it became the most prominent international aviation contest.

After the war, the competition was dominated for several years by sturdy flying boats clearly descended from military patrol aircraft. By 1923, though, the nature of the race changed to a contest between small, agile, and extremely fast aircraft, sponsored by wealthy individuals and organizations, and watched by most of the world.

The U.S. Navy had been competing in domestic air races for several years, and was doing well with modified designs intended for the fleet. In 1923 the Navy entered the Schneider with three variants of a quick little floatplane, the Curtiss CR-3. This sleek biplane used a Curtiss CD-12 liquid-cooled 465-hp engine to power a 2,747-pound (1,247kg) package, good enough to win against entries from France and England. Lt. David Rittenhouse, U.S.N., won the event for the United States with a speed of 177 mph (283kph); second place went to another CR-3 and a speed of 173 mph (277kph).

A period of intense public interest in aviation generally and in the Schneider Cup specifically marked the 1920s. Eventually the competition, previously sponsored by private flying clubs and organizations, was dominated by aircraft built at great cost by aviation companies and often supported by military units. Development and production money was mostly unavailable during the post–

Souvenir program from the final Schneider competition, 1931, when Britain retired the trophy.

29

Douglas World Cruiser with engine problems, Kanatak, Alaska, 1923.

30

World War I recession for anything related to flight—except for air racing.

By the late 1920s, the flying boats and biplanes had all disappeared, left far astern in the wake of tiny pursuit planes with huge engines and fragile structures. These engines were normally liquid-cooled monsters of 850 to about 1700 hp, with eight or twelve in-line jugs of prodigious displacement. As the power of these aircraft engines increased and their weight-per-hp declined, aircraft speeds improved rapidly. If a pilot and ground crew could keep the whole package together, they might achieve speeds in excess of 300 mph (480kph). The 1927 race was won with a speed of 271 mph (434kph); the next, in 1929, was won at 328 mph (525kph). By 1931 Schneider Cup racers were attaining straight-line speeds in excess of 440 mph (704kph), although not in the race itself.

Britain retired the trophy with a third win in 1931. The honors went to a Supermarine S6B, piloted by Lt. J. N. Boothman, a sleek floatplane that looked a lot more like a fighter aircraft than anything in the British or American inventories of the time. And when the Spitfire went to war a few years later, it and many other combatant aircraft used engines and lessons learned in competition for the Schneider Cup: lightweight airframes wrapped tightly around huge V-12 engines, the wing mounted low, and drag reduced to a minimum.

Prelude to War

Woodrow Wilson had proclaimed World War I "…the war to end all wars," and so it was … for a very few years. The Treaty of Versailles that finalized that war, however, set the stage for the next. Many Germans deeply resented those conditions and the global depression only amplified their resentment. Adolf Hitler capitalized on those resentments, beginning in the early 1930s.

On the other side of the globe, Japan's government was seriously preparing for the development of a colonial empire that would ultimately include much of Asia and the Western Pacific.

Newspapers and magazines of the time were full of reports on new military aircraft, weapons, and strategies developed by Germany, Italy, and Japan. These developments often included seaplanes and other aircraft. These developments clearly represented a threat, however distant, to U.S. interests, and the Army and Navy attempted to develop aircraft able to counter these threats. To do so, they approached companies that had provided aircraft during the recently concluded conflict, and other companies trying to produce aircraft for the new civil aviation market. One of these was Grumman.

The Grumman JF-1 and JF-2 Duck

Grumman was a new company in the early 1930s, and their first product was an amphibian biplane fighter designated FF-1. Patrol Squadron VF-5B got the first ones in June 1933. They worked well enough, but both the U.S. Navy and Grumman thought of the FF-1 as an interim design until something better came along.

At the time the Navy didn't have much money with which to buy airplanes, but it had some money for development, a situation that resulted in a great number of somewhat experimental designs issued to squadrons for test and evaluation. Like the rest, the FF-1 had some vices and some virtues. The virtues were combined with those of another patrol design of the time, the Loening OL, in a specification for a new design, designated XJF-1.

The XJF-1 was a heavy-looking plane whose central float had a pronounced duck-bill shape. The design seemingly learned nothing from the Schneider Cup competition, but it was the hottest machine in the fleet back then, with a top speed of 190 mph (304kph). The first flight of this new hybrid occurred in May 1933. After successful acceptance trials, the Navy ordered twenty-seven JF-1s and deliveries began in 1934.

Veteran pilots assigned to the new aircraft were delighted. It outperformed the

The catapult was believed to be the wave of the future for seaplane launches. Here, a successful test launch from onboard the U.S. Navy ship Maryland.

That's Jimmy Dolittle, back in 1925 when he was a lieutenant and was setting speed records in planes like this racer. He's just flown 232.57mph (374.2kph) in this little seaplane—a 600-hp Curtiss V-1400 engine occupies most of the fuselage.

old Loening utility airplane in nearly every category. Its rate of climb, top speed, and service ceiling were all about 50 percent better than the plane it had replaced. Its retractable landing gear made it a versatile aircraft for the Navy, now fully committed to supporting and integrating seaplanes and flying boats into the force.

The design began with a 700-hp engine, which was soon replaced by a 750-hp Pratt and Whitney R1820 Cyclone, the standard power plant for most Ducks. The final batch ordered from Grumman, however, specified a 850-hp engine, and the JF-1 built by the Columbia Aircraft Corporation used 1050-hp

Wright Cyclones. Even with the bigger engine, they were still slow.

Grumman Ducks would serve throughout World War II, flying for the U.S. Navy, Marine Corps, and Coast Guard. Most were unarmed and highly vulnerable to enemy fighters; even the Marine version, which carried machine guns and bomb racks, was still an easy target. They flew "plane guard" missions for carriers, recovering aviators who ended up in the water during landing and takeoff operations. Ducks flew long hours of antisubmarine patrol, photo missions, and pilot rescue, and shuttled personnel and cargo around the fleet.

The Vought OSU2-3 *Kingfisher*

Although unglamorous, the sturdy OSU2-3 Kingfisher was one of the most successful U.S. Navy aircraft of World War II, an observation airplane designed for service with the fleet. Launched from catapult rails on the ship's stern, Kingfishers worked primarily with cruisers and battleships. They were superb platforms to serve as the eyes of a task force, searching for enemy surface forces beyond the horizon.

Kingfishers rescued many downed pilots, including Capt. Eddie Rickenbacker, the famous World War I ace whose B-17 went down in October 1942. Rickenbacker's crew managed to get into their life rafts but were

A Vought OSU2-3 Kingfisher comes in for a landing, sending up a spray of water.

34

This 1918 Thomas scout plane was typical of attempts to adapt World War I land planes to the seaplane role.

not found until a Kingfisher crew spotted one of the rafts on November 11 and picked up four crewmen and the pilot. Rickenbacker and two other survivors were rescued the next day. The survivors made the aircraft too heavy to get off the water, so the pilot elected to taxi to the nearest secure island, 40 miles (64km) away, where he deposited Rickenbacker and the other crewmen, then took off for reinforcements.

While some Kingfishers were saving lives, other Kingfishers were taking them. Although the OSU2-3 could carry only a pair of 325-pound (148kg) depth bombs on wing racks, that was at times enough to damage a submarine, and the airplane's radio could provide accurate fire control for surface ships in the area. A pair of

Marine Kingfishers helped sink German submarine U-576 in July 1942 by directing naval gunfire from an armed merchant vessel, the *Unicol*, near Diamond Shoals, North Carolina. Another Kingfisher from Key West Naval Air Station's detachment at Cayo Frances attacked and damaged German submarine U-176 in May 1943, off the Bahamas, and called in a Cuban sub chaser to finish the job.

Kingfishers really weren't high-performance aircraft. The 450-hp engine meant that it was good only for 164 mph (262kph) tops, and normally cruised at about 120 mph (192kph). Service ceiling was just 13,000 feet (4,000m), but most of its patrol work was done down around 5,000 feet (1,500m) anyway. Empty, the OSU2-3 weighed about 4,100 pounds (1,900kg), and fully loaded it could barely get off the water at 6,000 pounds (2,700kg). Typical Kingfishers had a single .30cal fixed machine gun firing forward and another in a flexible mount for the observer to operate, but neither was likely to be very effective against any military target.

Despite its limitations, the Kingfisher was a popular scout plane throughout the 1940s and '50s. England bought many of them, -3 models the Brits called the Mk 1, and assigned them to the Royal Navy. These were sometimes launched from specially equipped merchant vessels and used to scout for submarines and enemy surface raiders. Some went to the Marine Luchtvaartdienst, the free Dutch Naval Air arm operating in the South Pacific, where they flew near similar aircraft operated by the Australian air force. Uruguay, the Dominican Republic, and the U.S. Coast Guard all used Kingfishers with great success.

The Boeing 314 Clipper

With interest in aviation strong during the Depression-era thirties, Juan Trippe of Pan

By 1925, when this photograph was made, the U.S. Navy had developed a serious interest in torpedo and bombing aircraft.

Following pages: A Navy CS patrol plane drops a torpedo, November 1926.

American Airways and others were busy developing international air routes across the Caribbean Sea and the Atlantic and Pacific oceans. In 1936 Pan Am issued a specification for a long-range four-engine flying boat for passenger and mail flights; Boeing's 314, a huge flying boat, was designed and built for this market.

The 314 first flew in June 1938 and classified as a commercial transport. With a wingspan of 152 feet (46m) and gross weight

of 84,000 pounds (38,100kg), it was a giant of its time. Intended for use on trans-Pacific flights, the 314 used 1500-hp Wright Double Cyclone engines and a wing and engine nacelle design borrowed from Boeing's new XB-15 bomber. Maximum range for the huge flying boat was an incredible 5,200 miles (8,300km).

Boeing named the plane after the fast-sailing ship of the mid-nineteenth century: the Clipper. On June 28, 1938, the age of the legendary Clippers of the air began with a

scheduled flight across the Atlantic, and within a few months other Boeing Clippers, in Pan American livery, were carrying wealthy passengers across the Pacific to Honolulu and on to Hong Kong. Within a few more months, the Pan Am Clippers were carrying people and mail between New York and Southampton, England; from Lisbon, then to Spain, down to Brazil, and across to Africa.

The fuselage of the new plane was tall and cavernous, with room for seventy-four passengers, dressing rooms, a dining salon, and a lounge. The food and service were superb, and the glamour of these premier long-haul carriers of high-priority cargo and important passengers captivated the era's media. At only an 184-mph (294kph) cruise speed, the passengers had plenty of time for dining, drinking, and socializing.

Twelve of the big Clippers entered service between 1938 and 1941, but their luxury days ended with the U.S. entry into World War II. Box lunches replaced the gourmet meals, and the comfortable upholstery was supplanted by folding troop seats. The Clippers routinely flew between San Francisco and Honolulu, getting high-priority passengers and cargo to the edge of the combat zone in one long day instead of a week and a half.

After the war, Pan Am put the Clippers back to work on trans-Pacific and transatlantic routes, but spare parts gradually made their operation more costly, and improved high-speed, high-endurance land planes like the Constellation made them gradually obsolete. The "Connie" chopped a third off the flying time on the trip from San Francisco to Honolulu when it replaced the flying boats on that run.

The US Mail goes aboard the Martin China Clipper, but not without a bit of ceremony.

The China Clipper westbound at about 2,000 feet (610m) above the new Golden Gate Bridge, November 22, 1935, on the first trans-Pacific flight.

A beautiful clipper soars above San fransisco Bay.

Pan Am's Yankee Clipper, a Boeing 314, could carry a profitable payload for 3,500 miles (5,600km).

Above: A look inside the hangar where a Short Singapore is under construction, 1926.

Left: Getting the big Clippers in or out of the water was a team effort.

Following pages: The Dixie Clipper lands at Lisbon, Portugal, on the first transatlantic passenger flight, June 29, 1939.

CHAPTER 3

Flying Down to Rio:

Transporting Passengers and Mail

The idea of long-distance passenger service by air was born in the years immediately following World War I. With an abundance of war-surplus bombers, many with cavernous flying boat hulls, fairly good load capability range, and dirt-cheap prices, aviation visionaries in Germany, France, England, and just about everywhere else got busy replacing bomb racks with wicker seats.

The Competition Heats Up

Soon enough, designers began experimenting with ideas for really big passenger aircraft, with really big capabilities. Most didn't work and some, like the great, grand Caproni Ca60, couldn't get off the water. This massive aircraft, with three sets of wings, eight 400-hp Liberty engines, and a forest of spars and wires—but no tail at all—was intended to accommodate a hundred passengers in style and elegance. It would have, too, if they were content to float around on the water, but the designer insisted on a flight test during which it barely got off the surface. During a second test, in March 1921, the pilot had difficulty controlling the beast and damaged it, and it was abandoned. But by this time a number of firms were getting into the seaplane act.

A BOAC Solent in flight, 1948. Production of the Solent kept flying boats in development and in service during the postwar period, particularly in the South Pacific and Australia.

Do X-1A, powered by twelve 525-hp engines, in flight, July 1929.

The Dornier J Wal

A much more practical design, and a remarkably modern one, came from Dornier in Germany, a giant designated the J but called the Wal (Whale). This superb aircraft set the standard for passenger aircraft for the next fifteen years. Armistice restrictions prevented Dornier from building the aircraft in Germany, so the company contracted for its fabrication in Italy. It was the first really successful passenger aircraft, operating all over Europe during the 1920s and into the '30s. Over three hundred Dornier Wal aircraft were sold to fledgling airlines in the Netherlands, Italy, Spain, Germany, and even Brazil and Japan.

The Whale could even be launched by catapult—and was, rather often. This system allowed the plane to cross the Atlantic, pausing mid-journey for a pit stop alongside a base ship, the *Westfalen* or the *Schwabenland*, designed for this mission.

Wals were used in transatlantic flight attempts, starting in 1924, and in daring exploration flights in Africa, South America, and the Arctic. A successful crossing of the south Atlantic was finally achieved in 1926 when Major Franco flew a Wal from Palos de Magues, Spain, over 6,200 miles (9,920km) down to Buenos Aires, Brazil. That flight took two and a half days of nonstop pilotage, a test of stamina for man and machine. Wolfgang von Grunau used another Wal—a well-used aircraft previously employed during an attempt to reach the North Pole—to fly from Germany all the way to Chicago in August 1930.

The Whale was quite an advanced airplane for its time, a sleek flying boat with a minimum of struts, tandem 600-hp V-12 engines, and a wingspan of 76 feet (23m). Those big engines with the low-drag design allowed the Wal to perk along at up to 140 mph (224kph) and cruise for almost 1,400 miles (2,240km) before refueling.

The Dornier Do X

The Dornier Do J was a successful aircraft although not an especially innovative one; it built on established design principles in a conservative way. But Dornier had grander ideas for what a long-range flying boat could achieve, and converted those concepts into metal with a giant airplane called the Do X.

In an era of flying boats, the Do X was more like a flying ship, a huge machine, long and slender as a cruiser, and nearly as big. Normally intended to carry up to seventy-two passengers in style and comfort, the X plane was ambitious for its time when it was designed and built in the late 1920s. It looked very much like a ship with wings instead of funnels, mounted high on the 131-foot (40m) hull just behind what would be the wheelhouse on a seagoing vessel. Above the 157-foot (48m) wing, mounted in tandem, were twelve Curtiss Conqueror engines.

Like a ship, the Do X had portholes instead of windows, and cozy little cabins for passenger privacy. Passengers could amuse themselves in the big lounge, listening to the gramophone or reading. There was a galley, too, and a bathroom, and a smoking room for gentlemen with their cigars and brandy. At

Seaplane travel was often quite luxurious, as evidenced by the spacious accommodations aboard the Dornier Do X.

mealtimes, passengers were summoned to a small dining room to be served by an attentive staff. It was a wonderful idea . . . with a few little problems.

First, the available engines simply were not quite equal to the challenge of getting this massive 123,000-pound (55,800kg) machine through the air with any kind of economy. They could get it airborne, certainly, and on one early flight the big plane lifted off with 169 passengers and crew aboard—including nine stowaways! That was an amazing feat for the time, and for many years afterward. But all those engines gulped fuel at more than 400 gallons (1,500l) per hour, and the throttles had to be advanced beyond their economical cruise settings. The tandem arrangement kept the aft engines from getting sufficient airflow to prevent overheating, and when they overheated, they lost power.

The throttles for the engines were under the control of the flight engineer, not the pilot, and those controls were well aft of the flight deck. When the pilot called for a power change, somebody had to run back through the radio room and the navigator's station and tell the flight engineer, an arrangement that is fine on a ship but is not desirable when cruising along at 100 mph (160kph), or taxiing up to a buoy.

Regardless of the problems, Dornier sent the big X boat on a grand tour to show it off to the world, and to demonstrate it to the long-haul airlines then just beginning service. The Do X left Germany on November 5, 1930, bound for Lisbon, Portugal, the Azores, and across the Atlantic to South America and ultimately home by way of the United States.

Unfortunately, the flight demonstrated the aircraft's deficiencies as well as its virtues. Heavy fog prevented the plane from

A surviving Sikorsky S-43 flying boat over hostile territory.

navigating all the way to Lisbon, so the pilot put the aircraft down on the ocean and taxied 60 miles (96km) into Bordeaux, France.

When the fog cleared they flew on to Lisbon, where a fire damaged a wing; repairs entailed a month's delay. Almost as soon as they embarked on their westward journey, the hull was damaged as they took off from Las Palmas, Canary Islands. Then, in order to make the 1,400-mile (2,240km) leg across the Atlantic, the craft had to be lightened and half of the crew and most of the elegant furnishings were removed. Even so, the Do X couldn't get much out of ground effect (the area close to the ground where a passing aircraft compresses the air slightly, normally providing a cushion during landing) and flew most of the crossing just 20 feet (6m) above the waves.

The Brazilians, who had been waiting eight months for this moment, were delighted. After some public relations flights up and down the Brazilian coast, the Dornier continued its epic flight northward, stopping at the West Indies and continuing on to New York City.

They arrived on August 27, 1931, to a hero's welcome, complete with a ticker-tape parade, medals, and speeches by politicians who discreetly avoided mention of the aircraft's slow progress. Then they all piled back in the big plane, the pilot sent a note to the flight engineer asking for full power, and off they went into the sunrise. After a stop for gas in Newfoundland, they pressed on back across the Atlantic . . . and ran low on fuel before arriving in Portugal. The skipper brought the Do X back down 6 miles (10km) offshore and taxied into port.

By this time it had become painfully obvious that the X plane was not quite ready for prime time. Two were sold to Italy but the high cost of operation made them unprofitable. The Italian Air Force used them for a while,

then scrapped both. The prototype survived until World War II—in a museum—but was destroyed in a bomb raid.

Sikorsky

About the same time, quite a few builders were introducing clean, reliable, fairly efficient flying boats into the long-haul passenger market. One of the best came from the brilliant mind of Igor Sikorsky and his Sikorsky Aero Engineering Corporation. Sikorsky had been an accomplished designer of four-engined seaplanes for Russia during World War I but escaped after the Revolution. His S-36 was a somewhat novel amphibian design, with its boat hull suspended from a high wing and with the tail attached by two tubular booms. Only five of this model were built (plus one experimental version for the U.S. Navy). One of these went to work for Juan Trippe's fledgling Pan American system and blazed the trail for Trippe's takeover of commercial air routes.

Sikorsky's next generation of flying boat, the S-38, was more practical and more successful. Two Pratt and Whitney 400-hp engines provided plenty of power for the ten-seat aircraft; it could take off and climb out with just one engine. This version appeared first in 1928, a slightly bigger plane with three times the range of its predecessor and impressive reliability. Only five of the civil version of the S-36 were sold by Sikorsky but 111 of the S-38s went into service with American Airways, Western Air Express, Pan Am, and Northwest Airways.

Trippe used the Sikorsky S-36—and the ethics of a shark—to take over the air routes all across the Caribbean as well as much of South America. Other operators used them to make exploratory flights in Africa and South America. These smaller flying boats set the standard for the big boats to come, and during the 1930s they started appearing from Sikorsky, Short, Martin, Supermarine, and Blohm und Voss.

51

A Short Brothers Calcutta sits dockside in 1930.

Above: The Short Brothers S-23 "C" class Empire flying boat first flew in July 1936.

Left: Short Brothers Shetland on its maiden flight, September 17, 1947.

Short Brothers

Short Brothers in the United Kingdom had been planning for long-distance passenger aircraft since the very early twenties with a preliminary design for a thirty-passenger flying boat to serve the far-flung empire. That empire was, in fact, beginning to become connected by air during the mid-twenties, and Short produced a tidy eighteen-passenger flying boat, the S-8 Calcutta, for this market. Imperial Airways was gradually building a web of support facilities and terminals across Europe, the Middle East, and far-off Australia and New Zealand. The first Calcutta flew in 1928, carrying passengers around the Mediterranean. Others followed, and the demand for air passenger service grew.

The demand for bigger, faster aircraft with longer range grew, too, and Short began producing a series of beautiful and efficient airplanes for this emerging market.

Above: A Short Brothers Canopus ready to take to the water for the first time, 1936.

Previous page: Short Brothers production line for Canopus flying boats, circa1936.

Even by air, a trip from England to the Persian Gulf in 1928 might take twelve days, with aircraft poking along around 100 mph (160kph), and stopping for fuel every 500 miles (800km).

Short produced the S-17 Kent flying boat in response, a four-engined flying boat with seats for fifteen passengers. Although the Kent was moderately successful, only three were built. But bigger things were on the drawing board.

Empire Flying Boats

In an attempt to speed up mail service within the empire, the British government subsidized an entirely new design for a long-range flying boat. The contract went to Short, including approval to begin production without bothering with prototype testing. Short's winning proposal was designated the S-23 "C" class, but before long was informally christened the "Empire" class. The first order was for fourteen huge flying boats, soon doubled.

These Empire flying boats were intended to accommodate comfortably twenty-four passengers and their baggage in addition to 3,000 pounds (1,350kg) of mail. Most had an 800-mile (1,300km) range, but three were designed for long-haul operations, with smaller payload but a range of 3,300 miles (5,300km).

Canopus, the first of the breed, lifted from the River Medway in July 1936. The second plane, Caledonia, was a long-range variant and flew in September. Both went into

Inside, the Short Brothers Canopus flying boat featured a spacious and high-tech flight deck.

service with Imperial Airways, with Canopus flying between Alexandria, Egypt, and Brindisi, Italy, in October 1936. Caledonia was soon operating between Egypt and Southampton, making the hop from Alexandria to a pit stop at Marseilles, France, in just eleven and a half hours, then on to

England in just another four and a half flight hours. Imperial Airways was soon serving Hong Kong, East Africa, Calcutta, Singapore, and Durban, South Africa.

Thirty-one of these handsome flying boats went into service and proved very successful. Nine more were built with bigger

engines and reinforcement, designed for long-haul operations. Of these, four could refuel in-flight for extreme range.

Empire flying boats fulfilled their mandate until World War II began, then served the RAF before being returned to commercial service. After the war, Empire flying boats continued on their original routes for several years until faster, longer-range land planes displaced them in the late 1940s.

Short-Mayo Composite

Even with the introduction of long-range passenger aircraft, there was a need for specialized, fast mail service across the Atlantic between England and Canada and the United States. An unusual solution was a two-stage rocket of an aircraft, the Short-Mayo Composite. Invented by Major R. H. Mayo, this system attached a small aircraft to a bracket on a larger one. The two took off latched together; when the journey was well along, the smaller plane was released to finish the flight. As awkward as the idea sounds, it worked pretty well in practice.

A pair of Short aircraft were used, a small S-20 Mercury four-engine floatplane and one of the big Empire S-21 flying boats, the Maya. Mercury could carry 1,000 pounds (450kg) of mail nonstop for better than 3,500 miles (5,600km), and Maya could carry the Mercury for several thousand miles before cutting it loose. Major Mayo flight-tested the idea with both planes in July 1938. The planes took off together, then Mercury was released out over the Atlantic, west of Ireland. Capt. D.C.H. Bennett flew the Mercury and a cargo of newspapers and news photographs all the way to Montreal, Canada, arriving twenty hours and twenty minutes after takeoff. They tried it again in October 1938, this time on a marathon journey from Dundee, Scotland, across the Atlantic all the way down to Orange River, on the coast of South America, almost 6,000 miles (9,600km). The flight took more than forty-two hours and set a record for seaplanes that hasn't yet been broken.

CHAPTER 4

Enemies in Flight:

The Seaplane in World War II

By the time the fighting began in earnest, in September 1939, seaplanes of all shapes, sizes, and capabilities were operating around the world. All the major combatants used them; some converted airliners and others designed for the business of combat. The Italians, Germans, and Japanese all had excellent fleets of flying boats and floatplanes. Britain, too, had some excellent designs. The United States, however, was slow to develop combat aviation of any kind and was busy trying to catch up when the bombs fell on December 7, 1941, at Pearl Harbor.

Blohm und Voss

German seaplanes are not particularly well known nowadays, but during World War II they were some of the best designs in service. These aircraft had some features and forms not often found on Allied aircraft—diesel engines, for example, and clean, tight lines quite unlike the era's competition.

The BV 138

The BV 138, a long-range reconnaissance design, evolved from a project begun in 1933. The aircraft was a sleek, up-rated version of the old NC flying boat, or the more recent Sikorsky S-36, with twin booms, a high wing, and a hull and fuselage slung below a pair of Jumo 206 diesel engines.

Martin PBM Mariners seldom flew such tight formations, except when they were being photographed. Instead, the Mariner normally operated alone on very long and lonely patrols over the open ocean.

Blohm und Voss made some of the prettiest and most capable seaplanes of World War II but nearly all were destroyed, in the air or on the water, by Allied fighters.

After a long gestation period, the 138 finally appeared in 1940 but still had some teething troubles. Soon enough, though, it went into service and quickly became a priority airframe. Some were used as troop transports during the Norway invasion; others were adapted to serve as mine sweepers, with huge dural loop antennas installed, powered by an auxiliary engine and generator in the fuselage. With a range of over 2,600 miles (4,200km), they were capable machines but were gradually abraded in the friction of air combat over Europe.

The BV 222

As good as the 138 was, the real champion in the Heavyweight Flying Boat competition during World War II was the Blohm und Voss BV 222 Wiking, the largest production flying boat to serve during the war. Originally intended for civil passenger transport across the Atlantic, the Wiking was commandeered by the Luftwaffe and put to work as a military transport.

Designed by a team led by Dr. Ingemar Vogt, the Wiking was initially expected to carry twenty-four day passengers, sixteen at night, at a maximum takeoff weight of 99,200 pounds (45,000kg). Instead, the 222s were stuffed to the gills with replacement troops and critical supplies, then sent across the Mediterranean to reinforce Field Marshal Rommel and his Afrika Korps. In this mode, the plane could absorb ninety-two combat-equipped troops and deliver them to an airhead more than 4,000 miles (6,400km) away. It could, and often did, come back with a full load of seventy-two wounded soldiers on litters.

These big planes were powered by six engines, normally twelve-cylinder-opposed Jumo diesels rated at 1000 hp. At full power the Wiking could plug along at about 242 mph (387kph) up at 16,400 feet (5,000m)—

not bad for a transport, but not fast enough to escape enemy fighters. Consequently, some had defensive armament, which added weight and drag and slowed them down; armed or not, the Wiking normally had two Bf110 fighters flying cover. During 1941 and '42, the Wikings routinely operated between Hamburg, Athens, and Derna in North Africa.

Fairey Swordfish

One writer referred to the British Swordfish as the "dinosaur" of all aircraft participating in World War II. If so the Fairey Swordfish Mk 1 was the favorite pet dinosaur of the Royal Navy's Fleet Air Arm. With all its struts and wires, this craft really did look like an airborne reptile, but its crews adored it. It certainly wasn't the only biplane in service —the United States, Germany, and Italy had others. The Swordfish, though, was a sin-gularly successful design, despite its prim-itive simplicity and obsolescent technology. Though a World War I airplane it had aged to perfection, and it sunk more enemy tonnage than any other Allied torpedo bomber of the war. It was called the "Stringbag."

The first prototype flew in April 1934 as a land plane, and soon went into produc-tion. It was designed and built by the Fairey Aviation Company Ltd as a two- or three-seat torpedo bomber and scout plane. Its engine was a 650-hp nine-cylinder radial. Wingspan was only 45 feet 6 inches (14m), length 36 feet 4 inches (11m)—a fairly compact design suitable for stowage aboard the small carriers of the day, or aboard cruisers or battleships. Full up, it weighed about 9,250 pounds (4,200kg), ready for takeoff with full fuel and weapons load. Maximum speed was about 140 mph (225kph), but that wasn't attained very often, except during attacks and when trying to escape enemy fighters; typical cruise was about 110 mph (175kph). Compared to many

other patrol and scout aircraft of the time, the Swordfish's endurance and range were somewhat limited.

Equipped with floats and stressed for catapult launches, the Swordfish proved to be remarkably successful at spotting for naval gunfire. On April 13, 1940, a single Stringbag launched from HMS *Warspite* directed gunfire against a force of seven enemy destroyers. Six of these ships were sunk by the gunfire, then the Swordfish took out the last ship with a bomb.

The type had many more successes, both as a floatplane and land plane. Nearly 2,400 were built and served through the end of the war.

Dornier

Some of the prettiest airplanes of all time, and certainly among seaplanes operated during World War II, must have been the Dornier Do 18 and Do 24. Originally intended for use by Lufthansa's transatlantic operations to South America, the Do 18 was Germany's entrant in the long-haul passenger market-place. The Do 18 was drafted into the war effort, but not before a specially modified aircraft set a new distance record for type of 5,215 miles (8,345km). Powered by two big, economical diesel engines—first 700-hp models, later with 880-hp versions—these planes were ideally suited to long-range patrol and search-and-rescue missions. More than a hundred Do 18s were built before production stopped in 1940.

The Do 18 was replaced by the Do 24, originally designed for use by the Dutch in the East Indies and then appropriated by Germany after the Netherlands was overrun in 1940. More than two hundred of this excellent design were built, utilizing three 1000-hp diesel engines on a wing mounted over the fuselage. The long, slender fuselage gave the plane the appearance of a submarine

The Dornier Do 18 resembled the PBY, but not because it was a copy; both planes were designed for very similar missions and those functions determined the aircraft's form.

with wings. Those clean lines and minimal drag allowed the Do 24 to cruise at better than 180 mph (290kph) and get up to 211 mph (338kph) in an emergency. Range for the Do 24 was a very respectable 1,800 miles (2,900km). After the Allies ejected German forces from France and the Low Countries, the surviving Do 24s were put to work by the French, some were sold to Spain, and a few were used by the Royal Australian Air Force.

Catalina

Of all the many types and models of aircraft designed and flown during World War II, among the most successful must certainly be the legendary Consolidated PBY, known then and now as the graceful Catalina. About four thousand Catalinas were built by the United States, Canada, and Russia, and the PBY saw combat service around the globe with the armed forces of many nations. It was such a durable and useful design that some are still working today. Sometimes described as the slowest aircraft of World War II, the Catalina was not a modern design but it was a proven one.

The design evolved from the wood and wire biplanes used by the U.S. Navy during the First World War and after. Its history goes all the way back to a 1928 develop-

ment contract for the Navy awarded to Consolidated. That experimental aircraft, designated the XPY-1, was the first large U.S. monoplane designed for operation from the water.

A refined design, the XP3Y-1, was the result, which the Navy ordered in 1933. It proved an immediate success when it flew two years later. With a "parasol" wing mounted above the fuselage on a pylon, the aircraft's unique appearance caught the attention of all observers. Out at the wingtips, the floats cleverly retracted, reducing drag and giving the aircraft a clean, elegant appearance in flight. In an era when air races and air records regularly made headlines, the big seaplane made some headlines of its own, establishing in 1935 a new long-distance record for seaplanes, flying from Norfolk, Virginia, to Coco Solo, Brazil, and across the United States.

The Development of the PBY

At that time the Navy was very frugal with aircraft contracts. With little support for combat aviation in the fleet, the consensus seemed to be that the next war would be fought by surface ships with large guns. But with its long range, high endurance, and ability to operate from the water, this new design captured the imagination of the top brass; a contract for sixty of the new

Sailors struggle to save a PBY after the first strafing attack by Japanese planes on 7, December 1941. The plane was destroyed later in the day by a second attack.

Above: The Ducks were still flying in World War II. These planes earned their names from the duck bill–like shape of their floats.

Left: A beautifully restored World War II Navy F3N-3.

planes, at $90,000 per copy, was issued in June 1935.

Deliveries began fifteen months later, and the sleek new aircraft showed potential not only for long endurance operations and extended range, but (with modifications) for excellent load-carrying capability. The Navy altered the design a bit with the introduction of wing-mounted bomb racks and gave the craft a new name, changing the designation from P3Y to PBY. "PB" indicated Patrol Bomber and the "Y" designation represented Consolidated, the manufacturer. Although Continental had been informally calling the new plane the Catalina, it was the British who first officially accepted this appellation. (In its typically conservative way, the U.S. Navy waited until 1941 to adopt the name.)

Patrol Squadron 61 (VP-6) got the first PBY and started wringing them out, operating from the sheltered waters of San Diego Bay's North Island. Typical of all aircraft evolution, the Navy and Consolidated just couldn't leave a good thing alone. As the PBYs started rolling out of the Consolidated factory in San Diego, there were more and more changes. The -1 versions got 900-hp engines instead of the 825-hp radials in the prototype. Both the -2s and -3s were ordered in 1936, and the -4 variant a year later. The first models used a

A Consolidated PBY-5A Catalina up on the step, just before take off.

sliding panel over the gun positions at the waist, but the -4 and all subsequent examples used large Plexiglas blisters instead.

The Catalina design was enthusiastically adopted by Canada, and hundreds were produced by Vickers (called PBV) and Boeing (designated PB2B) and delivered to the Royal Canadian Air Force. These were named the Canso. Others, designated OA-10, were delivered to the Army Air Force and used primarily for downed aircrew rescue. And the Navy's own Naval Aircraft Factory produced yet another variant during the war, an improved model called the Nomad. This version had a longer hull, stronger wing, more fuel capacity, and more tail fin surface —changes also incorporated into late model 6A variants produced by civilian factories.

Despite—or because of—the Catalina's slow speed, PBYs were among the very first aircraft in the U.S. inventory to be equipped with radar. The first sets were "metric" band sets; more capable "millimeter" band radars came later. These radars could detect a submarine running on the surface (as submarines of the time had to do) at night and through fog or rain.

Another innovative tool for the Cats was the Magnetic Anomaly Detector (MAD), a device that can sense the magnetic field of a submarine below the surface; the system is still used in refined form today. Coupled with the MAD were special dispensers for depth charges used on such aircraft, enabling the crew to drop weapons accurately on the first pass over the target.

The PBY in Action

By the summer of 1938, fourteen American squadrons were operating PBYs. The British bought one for test, liked it, and ordered hundreds more for the RAF's Coastal Command. Shortly after Germany invaded Poland and went to war with the British

A well-maintained World War II Consolidated PBY-5A Catalina in flight.

Commonwealth and France, the U.S. Navy ordered two hundred more PBYs for patrol duties in the Atlantic.

The PBY was an almost ideal aircraft for this mission, able to fly low and slow, and to stay out all day or all night. Those big blisters provided superb visibility for observers, and the racks on the wings could carry an effective weapons load for use against hostile submarines or smaller surface vessels. Although the Cat's basic crew was eight men, wartime patrols often consisted of twelve. The extras provided relief for pilots, observers, radio operator, and gunner on those long, long flights.

The British were putting these aircraft to good use while they were still being built. On May 26, 1941, a Coastal Command PBY

from 209 Squadron found the elusive German battleship *Bismark* after her daring run into the Atlantic and alerted surface units after they had lost contact with the ship. Another PBY took over the chase until a surface battle group caught up with the German vessel and sank it during an epic sea battle.

But these encounters didn't always work out with such success. A Coastal Command Catalina from Squadron 330, providing cover for Convoy QP-14, found and fought German submarine U-378 on September 21, 1942. Well equipped with highly effective antiaircraft guns, the subs began fighting back rather than diving when discovered on the surface. The Catalina was destroyed, but the crew survived and were all rescued by a Royal

69

A Consolidated PBY-5A seaplane awaits action on a quiet runway.

Navy vessel, the HMS *Marne*. Four other Catalinas would lose in fights with the submarines, along with at least sixty-one other patrol aircraft, before the Battle of the Atlantic was concluded in May 1945.

Although the Catalinas were a valuable addition to the antisubmarine warfare (ASW) mix from the beginning, it took a while before they and the other patrol bombers actually did much killing on their own. In fact, for the first two years of the Battle of the Atlantic, only two submarines were confirmed kills after aircraft attacks. By 1942, however, with better radar, weapons,

and tactics, that figure rose to thirty-one subs destroyed by patrol aircraft. According to one informed estimate, by the end of the war 220 German submarines were destroyed by patrol aircraft alone—but at the cost of some 700 patrol aircraft of all types shot down or shot up so badly that they were written off.

Although originally designed strictly as a flying boat, many Catalinas were built or converted to be amphibians, with retractable main and nose gear. This was extremely popular with American units but less so with the RAF, who ordered only

eleven of their seven hundred Catalinas with wheels.

One common application for the PBYs, particularly in the Pacific Theater, was the long-range, high-endurance recon mission scouting for enemy forces. Patrol Squadron 12—the legendary "Black Cats"—conducted antishipping attacks, particularly at night.

Catalinas equipped twenty-nine patrol squadrons early in the war, but more modern and capable patrol aircraft soon started replacing them. PBYs were relegated to search-and-rescue missions and to hauling cargo while PBMs and similar aircraft took over the

A Pilot Remembers

Capt. J. D. Mooney spent a career in the Navy, beginning before Pearl Harbor. He recalled his experiences in an interview with the author.

While I was going through flight school at Corpus Christi, Texas, in 1941, we were given our choice of aircraft for advanced training. I put in for the PBY, and got it. I was amazed how stable and easy it was to fly. One thing that made it easy was our instructors—most had fleet experience and knew the aircraft's characteristics quite well.

After a successful check ride and graduation, I was assigned to VP-92, a new squadron forming at Alameda, California. The aircraft carried three pilots, and as the "nugget," or new guy, I was assigned to be the Number Three pilot—which meant that I did all the navigating. But the patrol plane commander believed in rotating jobs within the cockpit, and so I started accumulating some experience flying the aircraft.

The squadron had just received PBY-5As, the amphibian version, and the experience of landing the aircraft on dry land was a new one for me. After five or six flights, the patrol plane commander let me bring it in on the runway. But it had a tricycle landing gear—one of the few U.S. planes of the war that wasn't a "tail-dragger"—and that helped make it very easy to land.

Finally, our orders came in and we were sent to the Atlantic. We ended up operating out of Casablanca, landing there the day after it was secured, in November 1942. We operated out of there for a long time, patrolling the approaches to Gibraltar and the Mediterranean.

We conducted long-range sweeps and searches for reported submarine sightings. If there was a convoy coming in from the United States, headed for the Straits of Gibraltar, we tried to meet it at our maximum range, just at dawn. Typically, just one airplane would provide cover for the convoy, and we stayed with them for "prudent limited endurance." That meant that it was up to the patrol plane commander to decide how long he could stay with the convoy before low fuel made him turn for home—not knowing for sure what the weather would be back at base.

We carried four 340-pound [155kg] depth charges in wing racks. These had hydrostatic fuses that could be set for any depth you wanted. Normally, we'd salvo them all at once, so two were set for shallow depth and two for deeper. . . . But the only submarines I actually saw were in the Caribbean. We had been escorting some ships hauling bauxite from British Guiana and were heading back to our base at Trinidad. It was a beautiful day, and we were flying at 9,000 feet [2,750m], higher than usual. There were no clouds and the sea was as flat as a mill pond. I looked out and saw a submarine not too far away and pointed it out to the plane commander.

We made a high-speed (for us) attack on it, but of course the sub saw us and "pulled the plug." Before we were halfway down, he had submerged. But we looked around and there was another out beyond the first, and then we saw two more, a total of four submarines! They were all about a mile from each other, and they were gone long before we could execute an attack.

That was one of the problems with the PBY—it was so slow on its approach, particularly from high altitude, that they would normally be gone before you could make a drop on them. It was a very comfortable airplane—but noisy. There was no sound-dampening insulation, and in the cockpit you sit just within a couple of feet of the propeller tips.

Endurance on the PBY-5A was not quite as good as the lighter -5 version, but I had some flights that lasted fifteen hours. The average was only ten to twelve hours. But we took flight rations along with us, and we always got the best food. And there was a hot plate, and you'd be surprised at how good some of the guys in back became at cooking during flight. There was always hot coffee aboard. And there were four bunks in back, so your crew could get some rest between standing watch as lookouts, which helped keep them alert. With missions that long, you got to know each other pretty well.

After a while overseas, I got orders to pick up a new Catalina in the States and report with it back to North Africa and VP-63. This was a squadron with a totally different mission—they were operating secret gear called the Magnetic Anomaly Detector (MAD). We were the first squadron to use it operationally. The skipper of VP-63 used the MAD-equipped PBYs to set up a barrier across the Straits of Gibraltar. We flew a racetrack pattern across the strait, trying to keep any submarines from getting in. Two planes flew the pattern at the same time, one on each end of the racetrack—each at 50 feet [15m] above the deck, pulling up to 100 feet [30m] for our turns.

It was a very successful technique. Just before I arrived, the squadron had three intercepts. We used another secret weapon with the MAD, something called a "retro bomb." This device used a standard "hedgehog" warhead attached to a 5-inch [12.5cm] rocket; the rocket would compensate for the speed of the aircraft and could put the weapon right on the spot where the MAD found a target. There were twelve of these weapons mounted on rails under the wing. They fired backwards off the wing, zeroing out the forward speed of the aircraft and dropping them right on the target. You had to be at exactly 110 knots airspeed for the technique to work, and you could set the system to work automatically—once armed, the rockets would fire instantly when the MAD registered a target below. The system worked well enough that the three attacks damaged the targets and British surface vessels moved in to finish off all three subs. One of these subs surfaced before sinking. The U-boat commander pleaded with the skipper to be told how he had been detected—he couldn't imagine how we had found him.

combat patrols. Still, in all its variations and in all its various missions, the Catalina was one of the most successful airplanes of the war. It might have been the slowest aircraft in the fight but, when the shooting was over, most of the four thousand built (including those built by Russia) were still flying. In fact, about forty or fifty PBYs are flying today. They are still durable, dependable, and slow, but remain the living legacy of a fine aircraft.

The PBY-6A

The late model -6A closely resembled its older siblings going back to 1938. Like them, it was intended primarily as a patrol aircraft, bomber, or torpedo plane, with search-and-rescue a secondary mission. Its wingspan was 104 feet (31.5m), length just under 63 feet (19m), and maximum height was about 22 feet 6 inches (7m). Empty and dry, the -6A weighed 21,480 pounds (9,750kg); full of fuel, crew, and weapons, maximum takeoff weight was 36,400 pounds (16,500kg).

Equipped with drop tanks, this Catalina could carry 1,778 gallons (6,756l) of 100/130 octane avgas, but 300 of those gallons (1,100l) were from external drop tanks. One hundred and thirty gallons (495l) of oil provided lubrication for the two Pratt and Whitney R-1830-92 turbocharged engines, each spinning a 12-foot (3.5m) Hamilton Standard propeller through a 16:9 ratio gearbox. The engines produced 1200-hp at 2700 rpm during takeoff, then were throttled back to 2550 rpm for cruise, generating 1050 hp at 7,500 feet (2,300m)—not quite enough power for this heavy version, according to most reports, for comfort.

Four machine guns protected this incarnation, two .30 cal Browning M1919A4s in the nose, each with a normal combat load of 2,100 rounds, and two .50 cal Browning M2 heavy machine guns in the waist mounts, with 1,156 rounds available for both.

Wing racks provided stowage for bombs, torpedoes, and depth charges. The craft could carry four 1,000-pound (450kg) or 500-pound (225kg) bombs, or twelve 100-pounders (45kg), or a pair of Mk13-3 torpedoes. For ASW missions, eight 325-pound (150kg) depth charges, set typically to explode at 25 to 50 feet (7.5–15m), could provide an alternative combat load.

The PBM Mariner

The PBY's cross-country flight got the attention of the U.S. Navy. As capable as the PBY Catalina was, it had many limitations. In an era of big Army Air Force bombers, the Navy wanted something similar, and the Catalina was too small for a useful bomb load and too slow to evade enemy fighters.

An obvious solution was an aquatic version of the big B-24, an aircraft with four powerful

engines, defensive .50 cal machine guns, armor, and self-sealing fuel tanks that would give it a chance to fight its way in and out of a target. A heavy bomb load and the new Norden bombsight would permit the Navy to conduct its own version of precision bombing. Four-engine bombers were expensive, so Martin developed a compromise for the Navy: a two-engine patrol bomber with more muscle than the PBY but at much less cost than the B-24. The result was the Martin PBM Mariner.

Martin didn't have a development contract, but in 1936 the company started work on the design anyway. Rather than build a full-sized aircraft, a quarter-scale flying version was fabricated, a miniature seaplane just big enough for a pilot and flight engineer. This model, the 162A, was used to test flight characteristics—and to sell the idea to the Navy. A full-sized aircraft was ordered in 1937 and flew two years later. The prototype began testing in 1939 and some modifications were made before production began.

Mariner Specifications

The PBM-5 is perhaps the best representative of the breed, since so many were built. With a wingspan of 118 feet (36m) and an overall length of just over 80 feet (24.5m), it was smaller than a heavy bomber, but bigger than the PBY. Twin R-2600 engines, each producing 1900 hp, provided a top speed of 211 mph (338kph). Empty and dry, the PBM weighed in at 33,175 pounds (15,060kg); fully loaded and fueled, maximum takeoff weight was 58,000 pounds (26,300kg).

The basic crew complement was eight or nine men, with accommodations for three or four more to provide relief on long missions; the extra crewmen served as relief pilots, gunners, and radio operators. These crews quickly discovered the Mariner's vices and

virtues. It was quite capable of twelve-hour missions, and its bomber variants packed enough punch to do serious damage to enemy targets. Unlike the PBY, there was room for the crew to stand up inside, to move about during the long flight. There was even a galley to prepare meals, and bunks for crew rest.

The PBM turned out to be 17 knots faster than the PBY-4, with considerably better range and payload. Although able to struggle up to 19,800 feet (6,000m), its rated service ceiling, nearly all Mariners did their flying down close to the water, where they belonged, and where they were safe from belly attacks. Top speed, therefore, is rated at 211 mph (338kph) at 1,500 feet (450m). Typical range, without auxiliary tanks, on patrol missions was a maximum of 2,240 miles (3,590km).

Mariners went in harm's way with a mixed bag of weapons, or none at all. The design included two .50 cal heavy machine guns in power turrets, intended to cope with enemy fighter attacks. Two more .50s were mounted in the waist, behind the wing, both in gimbal mounts, but aimed by hand. A fifth heavy machine gun was mounted in the tail to deter attacks from astern, and a .30 cal machine gun could be mounted under the tail, to cope with fighters making a belly attack. This was far more firepower than the PBY could offer with its two .50s and two .30 cal machine guns.

Bomb and depth charge stowage on the PBM was improved, too, inside internal bomb bays cleverly designed into the engine nacelles. This reduced drag and allowed a heavier load than the PBY, up to eight bombs or depth charges, the largest of which was a 1,600-pound (725kg) weapon. External wing racks were available for two torpedoes or four mines. And the nacelle bomb bays were plumbed to accept auxiliary tanks for long

Adding landing gear to the Catalina improved its versatility, but the added weight substantially degraded patrol performance.

A prototype Martin Mariner, the XPB2M-1, up on the step during testing.

ferry flights or reconnaissance patrols. Up to 12,800 pounds (5,800kg) of bombs, torpedoes, depth charges, or auxiliary fuel tanks could also be carried, but some carried eight .50s.

The Mariner at War

The first order for twenty-one aircraft started arriving in the patrol squadrons in 1940. Although war for the United States was officially more than a year away, the PBMs started antisubmarine warfare patrols almost immediately. Assigned to VP-55 and -56, the big new patrol bombers scouted for German subs, searched for survivors of torpedoed merchant vessels, tested British air-to-surface-vessel radar, and scouted for German outposts on Greenland and Iceland.

Patrol Squadron 55 (VP-55 in Navy parlance) was redesignated VP-76 in July 1941, and shifted operations to sunny Bermuda. There, on June 30, 1942, one of the PBMs equipped with the new British radar found, attacked, and destroyed a German submarine—the first of many such successes to come.

Many of the Mariners had their armor and power turrets stripped away and others had this equipment omitted during construction, making the aircraft lighter and extending the PBM's range. Some had their floors reinforced and were assigned to unglamorous but essential transport missions, hauling people and cargo around the Atlantic and Pacific theaters.

Nearly three hundred PBM-3C variants were tricked-out for combat patrols—three power turrets with twin .50s, two more .50 cal machine guns in the waist, plus the supersecret APS-15 radar for catching subs on the surface. This radar set was housed in a large dome directly behind the cockpit, on the upper surface of the fuselage. These C models equipped many patrol squadrons in the Atlantic, hunting subs as far south as Brazil.

Out in the Pacific, eleven squadrons equipped with D models did some hunting of their own. The D, with the Norden bombsight, attacked Japanese shipping, with torpedoes and bombs, often at low altitude, where the Norden was useless. Some units specialized in night attacks, known as "Nightmare" missions. Two squadrons of PBMs were committed full time to "Dumbo" missions, picking up downed aircrew in the open ocean.

But the aircraft tended to be under-powered and the R-2600-22 engines were difficult to maintain. The Navy intended to install bigger Wright R-3350 radials, but these were going into B-29s and there weren't any extras. Pratt and Whitney R-2800s were tried instead, found acceptable, and used for 628 PBM-5s. Providing extra power for difficult takeoffs in these -5s were JATO bottle mounts—rocket packs that, given the chance, could boost the Empire State Building off the ground. These late-model Mariners got a new radome, too, with advanced APS-31 radar inside.

After the war, the offensive mission of seaplanes generally and the Mariner in particular declined. Airfields were available just about everywhere, making the ability to operate from water less important than it had been before the war. A final variant, the -5A, was built as an amphibian and used for ocean rescue missions. Mariners equipped six squadrons, three each in the Pacific and the Atlantic. Some were sold to the Royal Air Force and the Royal Australian Air Force; the Uruguayan, Dutch, and Argentine navies; and a very few to private operators in South America for use as commercial airliners.

Sunderland

British aircraft design has always had its own distinctive, elegant style and one of the most stylish seaplanes of all time must be the British Sunderland. Big and powerful, the Sunderland was hugely successful—before, during, and after World War II. Sunderlands are pure flying boats, with no landing gear. The sleek design utilizes a tall, deep hull with a single step and a shoulder-mounted wing, well above the spray.

The Sunderland story began during the middle 1930s with an Air Ministry requirement for a long-range reconnaissance flying boat. The Short company developed the design, formally christened the S. 25 Sunderland, based on their already-successful S. 23 Empire flying boat, then in service with Imperial Airways. On October 16, 1937, the first Sunderland took to the air, the beginning of a nearly thirty-year career of service to British Commonwealth nations.

Wartime Sunderlands often had twin machine guns installed in a powered nose turret and another powered turret—this one with four machine guns—in the tail. The Mk II added a dorsal gun turret and ASV Mk II radar. All military Sunderlands could carry eight weapons, typically depth bombs, normally fused to detonate at about 30 feet (9m). These weapons were stored in the lower deck of the hull until the Sunderland was ready to attack; then crewmen moved the weapons through large doors in the side of the hull, out onto racks on the wings. A station for the bombardier was up in the nose, under the gun turret. During World War II Sunderlands slid down the ways with many variations of weapons and sensors—progressively better air-to-surface radar, more and bigger guns. Typical examples carried eight .303 cal light machine guns for close-in threats and a pair of .50 cal heavy machine guns for longer-range targets.

Mk V Sunderlands had four powerful guns in fixed mounts in the nose, aimed by the pilot. These were somewhat useful in combat with surfaced submarines, but the subs typically outgunned the Sunderland (and all other patrol bombers). The result was that Sunderlands sank some submarines, but submarines sank a few Sunderlands, too.

Mk I Sunderlands used four Bristol Pegasus XXII air-cooled radial engines rated at 1010 hp at full throttle. Mk IIs had more powerful Pegasus XVIII engines and constant-speed propellers. Mk Vs got 1200-hp Pratt and Whitney R-1830-90B power plants, complete with full-feathering props; the extra power and drag-reducing props meant that a Sunderland could stay aloft if German antiaircraft gunfire damaged two of the four engines. Ten big self-sealing fuel tanks in the wings held 2,552 gallons (9,698l), enough to keep the Sunderland in the air for about thirteen hours of patrol work.

The cavernous hull was divided into two decks, the upper one dedicated to the flight deck and cockpit positions, the nose gunner's station, and the flight engineer's console. Down below was a small ward-room, a weapons storage station, a small galley for meal preparation, an electric tea kettle, two Primus stoves, and an oven. There were also bunks for two men, a "loo," sink, and shaving mirror. Crewmen often had to spend extended periods aboard Sunderlands and they naturally customized their mobile apartment with dishes, curtains for the portholes, and a battery-powered radio. Presumably they also managed to find some additional bunks.

Thirty-four Sunderlands were in service when war began for England in 1939, but many more were built during the war—ninety Mk Is, forty-three Mk IIs, 456 Mk IIIs, and 150 of the final version, the Mk V, for a total of 739. The Mk IV variant, the Seaford, itself became a unique aircraft, intended for work in the Pacific, but only six were manufactured.

After the war, British Overseas Airways Corporation took over some of the Sunderlands, converting them back to service as long-haul airliners. Twenty-one were modified to Hythe-class Sunderlands, luxury passenger planes with seating for just twenty-two. Sandringham-class Sunderlands, with accommodations for forty-five, served Johannesburg, South Africa, Singapore, and Japan. Others served major cities in Scandinavia, Australia and New Zealand, South America, and Africa.

Mars

Like other designers of seaplanes, Glen Martin was fascinated with the idea of large, long-range aircraft. The Mars grew from a 1938 U.S. Navy order for a single large patrol bomber. As Martin imagined the aircraft, it would be a kind of flying battleship, able to carry huge quantities of weapons and warriors. According to Martin, it was to have multiple gun turrets and racks for the biggest bombs.

Martin promoted the idea of this long-range dreadnought of the air in speeches and articles. He claimed that a single Mars could deliver by itself enough soldiers and ordnance to capture a small enemy island. He predicted that the Mars could carry enough bombs to devastate a shipyard or rail center—alone, on a single mission. He even claimed that a squadron of the big seaplanes could bomb Tokyo into rubble—in a week.

The prototype Mars (as it would be called) was designated XPB2M-1. Begun in August 1940, it was ready for flight in November 1941. A propeller failure during taxi tests threw a blade, though, and the Mars caught fire. It was quickly extinguished, but the damage to the starboard wing and number-three engine took six months to repair.

While the repairs were being made, the Navy had second thoughts about this battle-ship of the sky. Carrier-launched aircraft did an excellent job of bombing enemy targets and were already flying those missions.

Bombs away! A huge Martin Mars unloads during a demonstration water drop.

Development of the Mars was modified to a kind of airborne truck, able to haul huge payloads across vast distances. When the Mars finally went to war, it was hauling cargo. The gun turrets were removed and the Navy rechristened the plane the JRM.

Only seven were built, including a prototype, but they could haul 10 tons (9t) of cargo from San Francisco to Hawaii, or three hundred passengers, or up to about 19 tons (17t) of cargo on resupply runs to distant outposts in the Pacific. After World War II, the Mars flying boats continued to serve the Navy until 1956. During their years of service, they logged 87,000 hours without accident and set many records for endurance and lift capability, some of which still stand.

Rod Bittencurt served as a radioman on Mars boats during the 1950s, flying from San Francisco Bay to Hawaii. It was a thirteen-hour run, departing at 9:30 at night and timed to land at 8 A.M. local time. Mars ships were moored at Alameda, but had to be taxied far down the bay to get into position for the takeoff run into the prevailing wind. One of Rod's duties was to perch in the forward gun hatch, inspecting the water ahead of the taxiing Mars and warning of drifting logs and other hazards to navigation.

Most of the flights were long and uneventful, but the takeoff run was tricky. Pilots had just sixty seconds to get the heavy plane up on the step, get it unstuck, and get it airborne. Then they made a left turn, avoiding the Oakland Bay Bridge, maneuvering the still-slow Mars around downtown San Francisco, and turning west, toward the open ocean and gathering night. The radio operator sent in a report every half hour.

Mars Operations Today

Two of the original six production aircraft are still flying, half a century after they were designed and built—the Philippine Mars and the Hawaii Mars. Both are air tankers used to fight forest fires in Canada.

Their second career is an interesting one. While nearly all World War II military aircraft have been melted down or installed in museums, the two surviving Mars craft continue to work hard for a living. They have been converted to drop water or fire-retardant foam on forest fires. The water pickup is done directly, at 70 knots. The pilot skims across the water, with the hull up on the step, and one of the flight engineers opens a scoop. Ram pressure quickly fills the tanks at the rate of about 2,000 pounds (4,400 kg) of water a second. When the tanks are filled, after only about twenty-five seconds, the scoops are closed and takeoff power applied.

Once airborne, borate foam concentrate is added to the 7,200 gallons (27,350l) of water. Taking his orders from the "fire boss," the aircraft commander will be given a target for the drop. Flying at only 150 to 200 feet (45.5–60m) above the terrain, through smoke and the sometimes severe turbulence generated by the heat of severe forest fires, the Mars delivers its load on the fire—not exactly the kind of bombing mission Glen Martin had in mind sixty years previously when the Mars was designed, but one he might be happy with just the same.

The Martin Mars JRM was the largest aircraft in the U.S. inventory until the B-36 came along, and it is still a big aircraft—200 feet (60m) from wingtip to wingtip, 120 feet (36.5m) long, and 48 feet (14.5m) high. During military service, the Mars used the then-largest aircraft piston engines made, Pratt and Whitney R-4360 Wasp Majors for the RJM-3, the last variant of the breed. The surviving aircraft have been reengined with Wright Cyclone R3350-24WA power plants, each producing a maximum of 2500 hp and turning four-bladed propellers over 15 feet (4.5m) across.

Typical of a big, heavy aircraft, the Mars slides back down to earth at 115 mph (184kph) and should touch down at 92 mph (147kph). Fuel consumption is 337 gallons (1,280l) per hour at cruise, 190 knots. During fire operations, that consumption goes up to 780 gallons (2,965l) per hour, although the aircraft will be flying at 138 knots. Hawaii Mars can carry about 6,500 gallons (24,700l) of fuel, Philippine Mars about twice as much, 13,200 gallons (50,200l).

Kawanishi

So what was the best seaplane of World War II? According to many aviation historians, the short list has to include Japan's Kawanishi Type 2, known to the Allies as "Emily," a big flying boat with superb all-around performance.

The Type 2 came off the drawing board in 1938, as Japan built up her military forces for anticipated campaigns, as a replacement for the older Type 97 flying boat. Intended for long-range patrol and bombing missions, the requirement called for 30 percent more speed, 50 percent more range, and much better maneuverability. Kawanishi's solution was a big, high-wing design, powered with four large radial engines, a deep hull, and lots of guns pointed in every direction. Retractable landing gear allowed the big plane to operate from land or water.

There were some typical growing pains, the same sort of thing that delayed the introduction of British, Russian, and American flying boats—such as a tendency to "porpoise" while taxiing, and some problems with control at low speed. But the hull bottom was eshaped and the vertical fin enlarged, and the Type 2 Flying Boat Model 11 (as they officially called it) was approved for production in 1941.

The first examples used four big 1530-hp Mitsubishi Mk4A Kasei 11 radial engines,

An old World War II Short Sunderland, still flying.

The Japanese "Emily" sported defenses that made Allied fighter pilots nervous.

but those were later replaced by huge 1850-hp Kasei 22 models. The tremendous power of these engines, combined with the excellent aerodynamics of the design, made the Emily the fastest flying boat of World War II, with a top speed of 290 mph (465kph) at 16,400 feet (5,000m).

Emily had the speed to run from some adversaries, but also possessed the firepower to fight it out when necessary. Five 20mm cannon and three 7.7mm machine guns provided a protective screen that made assaults on the big flying boat dangerous; Allied fighter pilots attacked with care and caution. Self-sealing

fuel cells and armor plate for the crew made the Emily hard to kill even when hit.

Equipped with surface-search radar and a weapons load of two 1,764-pound (801kg) torpedoes or eight 550-pound (250kg) bombs, the Type 2 was a very formidable attack bomber. Her combat debut was a three-plane mission against Pearl Harbor, a 2,000-mile (3,200km) flight from Watje in the Marshall Islands, in March 1942. With a maximum combat range of about 2,900 miles (4,650km), the Type 2 aircraft could not complete the mission without refueling, so they rendezvoused with a specially equipped sub-

marine off French Frigate Shoals to take on extra gas. The flight then took off, flew the remaining 650 miles (1,040km) to the target, and then discovered that the whole island of Oahu was obscured by heavy cloud. They returned without dropping their weapons.

One hundred sixty-seven Emilys were manufactured. Most were patrol bombers but thirty-six H8K2-L models were adapted to serve as fast passenger and cargo planes. These were called Seiku or "Clear Sky" variants, with just one 20mm cannon and seats for up to sixty-four passengers. Normal crew for the Emily was ten men, most of whom were gunners. The cannon were installed in the nose, tail, and dorsal turret, with machine guns mounted in the waist aft of the wing.

In spite of all that firepower and speed, all but one of these Kawanishi Type 2 flying boats were destroyed during World War II. The sole survivor was captured after the fall of Japan and brought to the United States for study.

The Kawanishi was a great airplane, but not great enough to fight off the swarms of Allied fighters that hunted the big flying boat whereever it flew, and picked them off, one at a time. The Type 2s took a toll on the attackers, but went down in flames or were destroyed on the deck. The Allied campaign against Japanese air and naval forces built from a weak, puny force in 1942 to an irresistible onslaught by 1945. One hundred and sixty-six Kawanishis, along with thousands of other excellent Japanese aircraft, were ripped apart by machine-gun and cannon fire.

Probably the best flying boat of World War II, the Japanese "Emily" was fast, with excellent range and tremendous firepower This is the sole survivor.

CHAPTER 5

The End of an Era:

Military Applications After the War

By 1945 a web of air routes, landing fields, and support facilities had been developed around the world, most intended for wheeled aircraft. The primary virtue of the seaplane—the ability to operate from almost any bay, lake, or inlet—was no longer very important. No matter where you went in the world, some sort of airfield was likely to be nearby. Consequently, interest in large seaplanes declined rapidly. But before seaplane technology was abandoned for most military and commercial applications, a few intriguing designs were tried.

Several interesting models were developed soon after the Second World War for use by the U.S. military, and, in one famous instance, progress was actually spurred when the government began to lose interest in the project.

The Spruce Goose

Back in the dim, dark, early days of World War II, submarines were taking a tremendous toll on maritime commerce in the Atlantic. Henry Kaiser's shipyards turned out Liberty ships at a rate of one a day, but that wasn't fast enough to keep up with the British war industry's demands for American materiel.

No, it's not a joke, but a Mariner on experimental floats during 1963 trials. The vertical floats allowed the aircraft to float on station and conduct antisubmarine sensor operations isolated from the ocean swells. The aircraft's flight characteristics, though, must have been interesting.

83

Flight engineer's station (right) and copilot's seat (left) aboard the Spruce Goose's flight deck.

Kaiser came up with a lot of good ideas; one of them was a huge aerial freighter that could rival a Liberty ship's capacity and provide an aircraft's speed.

The design was first named the HK-1, honoring Howard Hughes (then an accomplished aviation pioneer) and Kaiser. Funded by the U.S. government, the development program was slow. Aluminum wasn't allotted to the HK-1, so the design was instead based on laminated wood construction. Although the aircraft would later be known as the Spruce Goose, it was actually made mostly of birch veneer..

Every other American design of the time was dwarfed by the concept and ultimate construction of this massive airplane. With a wingspan of almost 320 feet (98m), it was bigger even than today's Boeing 747s. Eight of the most powerful engines of the day, Pratt and Whitney R-4360s—the most

Ground crew personnel make ready to drop mooring lines just before moving the H-4 out into open water.

Hughes's H-4 Spruce Goose was actually made mostly of birch, like many other successful designs of World War II.

The huge Hughes H-4 under tow in Long Beach harbor, 1947.

powerful radial reciprocating engines ever
built—provided 3000 hp each. Together,
that 24,000 hp could move the huge aircraft
at 200 mph (320kph) for twenty hours at a
time. With a gross weight of about 400,000
pounds (182,000kg), the plane was the
biggest built to that time, and so it remains,
even in the day of 747s and C5 Galaxies.

Yet, as with many other development
projects during the war, priorities changed
once work had begun. Funding went to other
projects and the HK-1 languished. Then
critics claimed the design was a boondoggle,
that it wouldn't and couldn't fly. One U.S.
senator called it a "flying lumberyard." The
government brought suit against Hughes.

It took some time, but Hughes finished
the aircraft—with his own money.

On November 2, 1947, Hughes took
the completed H-4 (as it was rechristened)
out into the harbor at Long Beach, California,
for taxi testing. As Hughes completed his
tests, he applied full takeoff power to the
eight engines. The aircraft came up on the
step and rose into the air. Hughes held it
there for about a minute, skimming across
the harbor at about 70 feet (21m) and about
80 mph (128kph). Then he reduced power
and brought the plane back down. As it
happened, that was the one and only flight of
the huge plane, but it proved Hughes's point:
the aircraft was quite airworthy, and the
critics finally shut up, at least for a while.

The Convair R3Y Tradewind

One exciting aircraft that evolved from the
large World War II transports was a design
that could have been quite successful but
didn't quite make it: Convair's Tradewind, a
large flying boat.

The Tradewind first flew in early 1950.
Four Allison XT-40-A-4 engines provided

The bulking Spruce Goose under construction, 1946.

Convair R3Y-2 just after takeoff.

5850 hp each, driving counterrotating propellers. Those engines were mounted on top of the 145-foot (44m) straight wing, itself mounted high on the tall fuselage. The cockpit was installed on top of, rather than inside, the 140-foot (42.5m) hull area, giving the aircraft a long, unobstructed cargo compartment. This layout permitted the Tradewind to taxi right up to the beach, drop its ramp, and then dispense its vehicles directly onto dry land in a fast and efficient manner.

The Tradewind was the only turboprop-powered flying boat accepted by the U.S. Navy. It was fast, with a top speed of 388 mph (621kph). The Navy originally wanted it

for patrol duties, but when the program was delayed by engine vibration problems, the mission was converted to transport. That trick bow ramp earned it the nickname Flying LST, after the landing craft with the same feature. Only twelve were built.

The Martin P6M SeaMaster

Among the kinkiest aircraft designed during the post–World War II period (and there were a surprising number of kinky experimental aircraft) was Martin's big, beautiful P6M SeaMaster. With its sharply swept wings and

four Allison J-71 turbojets, this sleek flying boat's design was far ahead of its time. The plane used Martin's tested-and-true big hull and high-mounted wing design, with the engines safely out of the spray. But, unlike Martin's traditional layout, the long wings drooped so far that they almost touched the water. A crew of just four managed the aircraft's duties, primarily mine-laying and reconnaissance.

The Seamaster flew first on October 10, 1955, and performed well enough that the Navy ordered thirty of them. With 600 mph (960kph) as a top speed, it had the potential for dropping nukes and has been called a

The Martin YP6M-1 SeaMaster was a radical design, but by the time it finally took to the air it was already obsolete.

antisubmarine warfare, and the Dash-1s were stuffed with electronic sensors and communications gear. Production models came along in 1951, just in time to help patrol the Korean War combat zone.

An improved version, the P5M-2, took off a couple of years later and became an instant hit. Pilots said it had the best hull of any flying boat for rough-water operations. Its radar and sensor suites were powerful and reliable. The Marlin's 2,000-mile (3,200km) range permitted effective patrols. And when supported by a Navy seaplane tender, the Marlin could set up shop far from base and operate independently for months.

Marlins would be used extensively in Vietnam, patrolling the long coastline and looking for North Vietnamese infiltrators. Such small ships and fishing boats mixed easily with the hordes of innocent routine maritime traffic, then would sneak ashore to unload weapons and soldiers under cover of night. They were very hard to catch, but the Marlin's big radar and the experience of her crew helped distinguish the bad guys from the good guys.

Most patrol work, however, was quite dull. Military aviation is reputed to be "hours and hours of boredom, punctuated by moments of sheer terror," but one former Marlin crewman has stated, "Most flying boat activity was merely long hours of boredom without the short periods of sheer terror. Just the boredom."

The end of the line came on November 6, 1967. Commanders Smolinski and Surovik from VP-40 at North Island, California, fired up a Marlin, taxied out into San Diego Bay, turned into the wind, and applied full throttle. The aircraft climbed up on the step, then lifted off the water for a final, ceremonial flight. That was the last operational flight of any U.S. Navy seaplane, and the end of more than fifty years of service.

92

A Martin P5M-2 Marlin decked out in French Navy colors.

"seagoing B-52." The P6M included a rotary bomb bay with racks that could be used several ways—to drop mines, bombs, or other weapons, or to expose recon cameras. The Navy bragged that the SeaMaster could attack Soviet subs in their home bases and mine the Black Sea.

Testing went well until one of the prototypes had a bizarre control failure. The horizontal stabilizer actuator inadvertently went to full travel while the aircraft was at cruise. The plane pitched forward sharply and the engines ripped away from the wings. Then, under the tremendous air loads, the wings bent so far that the wingtips actually curved around the hull and touched. All three crewmen were killed.

Then the second prototype aircraft had a similar control failure, pitching up in a loop before coming unglued. This time, fortunately, the crew used a new escape hatch to abandon the aircraft and survived. A major redesign followed, with conventional wind dihedral instead of the original anhedral, more powerful engines, and a new flight control and autopilot system based on the then-new transistor technology.

Twenty-four aircraft had originally been ordered, but the crashes and delays bumped up the cost of the program. The order was trimmed to eighteen, then twelve. The Navy talked about operating them as a single specialized squadron. Finally, in 1959, the Navy canceled the program.

Martin Marlin

Martin's Marlin has the sad distinction of being the last flying boat operated by the U.S. Navy. The initial version, the P5M-1, first flew in 1948. It had a long, slender hull with small frontal area for its bulk, reducing drag. Its mission back then was primarily

The Martin P5M served the U.S. Navy from 1952 until 1966, mostly in the western Pacific.

Above: A prototype version of the amphibious model Catalina, the XPBY-5A, drops its gear and wingtip floats for the camera, November 29, 1939.

Opposite:Canadair's very successful amphibian firefighter, the CL-215.

CHAPTER 6

Russia Revealed:

Beriev Seaplanes

Just when it seemed that the last of the commercial flying boats had flown off into the sunset, along comes the Russian aviation industry with a modern, midsized amphibious jet transport, the Beriev Be-200. Actually, Beriev and other Russian design bureaus had been pumping out flying boats, floatplanes, and amphibians for many years. Not much was heard about Russian aviation until the Cold War finally thawed, and ever since then aviation addicts have been delighted with revelations about this parallel universe and its fascinating products.

The Beriev Design Bureau

Beriev has been building seaplanes since the 1930s, when it was formed by Georgii Mikhailovich Beriev in the town of Taganrog, near Rostov on the Azov Sea. Russian design bureaus function very much like Western independent corporations, despite their (former) ownership by the government. They were all led by imaginative, forceful individuals with a clear vision of what could be done with an airplane. In the late thirties Beriev came up with a great design for a little seaplane, the MBR-2, a short-range flying boat. Over 1,500 MBR-2s were built and used extensively during the Second World War. They continued to serve for many years, until the design was finally retired in the late 1950s.

Two Beriev planes fly tandem: a Be-12 in a tight formation with an A-40.

On the side of a modern Russian seaplane, bright graphics provide identification.

After the war, as tensions between the Warsaw Pact nations and NATO simmered ominously, Beriev produced another important design, a long-range patrol plane first designated LL-143. This aircraft, which appeared in 1947, was a contemporary of the Martin PBM Mariner, with many of the same missions and configurations. The LL-143 used the same gull-wing layout, for the same reasons—to get the piston engines up out of the spray. During the test and evaluation process Beriev modified the sensors, power plants, and weapons systems for the new patrol plane, then gave it a new name: the Be-6. The first production Be-6 flew in 1949; about 150 more followed, and NATO assigned it the name "Madge." Most were used within Russia, but about twenty went to work for the Chinese Navy.

The Be-10, an elegant although not very successful attack flying boat, followed in 1956. This big combat aircraft had wings and tail swept back at extreme angles, and a pair of Lyulka AL-7RV turbojet engines installed at the base of the wings. Only twelve were built.

The Be-12

About this time, the Soviet Naval Air Force (properly, Aviatsiya Voenno-Morskovo Flota, or AV-MF) issued a request for a new patrol plane with advanced submarine hunter-killer capabilities. NATO had been busy during the 1950s developing the Polaris missiles and the George Washington–class submarines to deploy them. These missiles had to be launched fairly close to their targets—and those targets, as everyone knew, were in the Soviet Union. In the context of the time, the threat was extremely dangerous, and to counter the NATO threat, Beriev designed the Be-12.

This amazing aircraft first flew in 1960, but by all measures and according to Western military analysts at the time, it was already obsolete. Its first public appearance was at the Soviet Aviation Day show at Tushino, just outside Moscow. Western military attachés made note of it but were not particularly impressed. The era of the flying boat patrol plane was supposed to be over, and NATO forces were converting to land planes like the P-2 Neptune. NATO christened the Be-12 "Mail." Russians started calling it "Tchaika" (Seagull) because of the distinctive wing form. The factory at Taganrog began building the Be-12, first at ten per year, then fifteen per year after 1967. One hundred thirty-two Seagulls were built, the last coming off the line in 1973.

The Be-12 turned out to be a much more important aircraft than expected. Loaded with the latest in Soviet sensors, including an advanced 4.5m (15-foot) Magnetic Anomaly Detector (MAD) mounted as a "stinger" at the rear, a capable surface search radar in the nose, and weapons racks on the wings and inside a fuselage bay, the Be-12 was a bear looking for hunters. It was used for ASW, search-and-rescue, antishipping patrol, photo survey, cargo and passenger transport, and for breaking records.

The Be-12 holds every single record for planes of its type—forty-four classifications for amphibians and flying boats: climb to height records, loaded and empty, speed records for 300km (185 miles) and 500km (310 miles) closed course, with and without payload, and around a 1,000km (620 miles) closed course. It has been setting records since 1964, the latest in 1983, and is unchallenged within its class.

The Be-12 is powered by two 4120-hp Ivchenko AI-20D turboprop engines, each installed on top of the narrow cord wing. Ground crew can use the clamshell cowlings as maintenance platforms, an important convenience during servicing. Eleven thousand

The Beriev Be-12 has an unusual appearance, but then it is an unusual aircraft; it holds forty-four world records for its class.

liters (2,900 gallons) of fuel storage in internal wing tanks keep the plane aloft for a long time. Weapons load is an impressive 3,000kg (6,600 pounds) and, thanks to hatches built into the fuselage, the bays and racks can be loaded with the aircraft on the water. Those weapons include homing torpedoes, depth charges and bombs, sonobuoys, flares, and markers used mostly for attacks on submarines. Typical of many Russian patrol aircraft, the Be-12's nose is glazed, providing a great view for the bombardier or observer.

Typical crew for Be-12 missions is five or six men—pilot, copilot (who doubles as radio operator), navigator, an electronics specialist, and one or two ASW sensor operators.

Here comes the new breed of seaplane: Beriev's new Be-200 multi-purpose amphibian, with gear down and locked.

The Beriev Be-200

As Communism was discarded in favor of a market economy during the 1990s, Russian society experienced radical changes. For the aviation industry, this conversion produced tremendous problems as well as new opportunities. Design bureaus like Beriev suddenly had to fend for themselves, and come up with models that could compete with their Western counterparts on the open market.

One opportunity the market seemed to offer was a need for medium-range passenger and cargo aircraft to serve the Pacific Rim nations. Many of these countries have long, rugged coastlines with little room for conventional airports, but lots of bays and estuaries suitable for seaplane operations. Beriev designed a new aircraft to serve this market, the first new Russian design since the collapse of the Soviet Union, and the first new commercial flying boat in many years.

The aircraft looks quite similar to a conventional jet twin, except that the engines are mounted high on the wing roots, rather than below the wings or back on the tail. The fuselage is quite conventional in form, even though it forms a watertight, two-step hull. It can operate from any Class B airport (1,800m [5,900 feet] runway) or waterway at least 2m (6 ½ feet) deep and with waves no more than 1.2m (4 feet).

Allied Signal, an American company, helped develop avionics for the Be-200, and the whole aircraft is designed for the requirements of the world marketplace. That includes provision for installing British Rolls-Royce BR-175-53 or American Allison GMA-2100 engines. It also includes designing the aircraft to comply with the American FAA's FAR-25 airworthiness standards; clearly, Beriev wants to have the Be-200 certified for operation in the United States.

Like many other modern commercial aircraft, the Be-200 is designed to be a quick-change artist, convertible to several applications. One important role within Russia is for fire fighting, as the Be-200 can scoop water during high-speed taxi. Another is as a passenger transport, for which it can be configured with sixty-four seats for economy passengers, or thirty-two business class, or eighteen executive passengers.

The Be-200's first flight occurred in September 1998, a thirty-minute hop with K. V. Babich as pilot in command. Beriev had orders for ten aircraft before the first flight and promises of orders for another sixty to seventy-five from Russian agencies. Another twenty or so orders are forecast from European operators.

101

The Beriev A-40 Albatross is another new Russian seaplane, first displayed at the Tushino airshow in 1989. This one is taxiing up the ramp after a mission.

CHAPTER 7

Still Flying After All These Years

Although not as common or as widely sought as in earlier decades, seaplanes today are still very much in demand and still in production. Two important contemporary uses are found in the field of fire fighting and in bush transport, both of which utilize some of the seaplane's unique characteristics to accomplish demanding and highly specialized tasks.

Canadian Contributions

Canada has always been an important market for marine aircraft and has contributed many excellent designs to aviation over the years. Bombardier Aerospace is still manufacturing an excellent amphibian, the Canadair 415. Quite a few important designs have come from the de Havilland Aircraft of Canada Ltd. So well suited have these aircraft been that the United States Army opted to purchase Caribous, Buffaloes, Beavers, and Otters by the hundreds during the 1960s, in favor of U.S. designs.

The Canadair 415

Based on the CL-215, Bombardier's earlier successful amphibian used for fire fighting since the 1970s, the 415 is designed and configured specifically for that purpose.

One of the most adaptable and accessible seaplanes, the Kit Fox (shown here in the skies above Idaho) can be fitted with floats or skis.

104

This de Havilland D460M seems to sail above blue waters.

The development program began in 1991, the first plane flew two years later, and deliveries began in 1994. With a wingspan just under 94 feet (28.5m), length 65 feet (20m), and maximum takeoff weight of about 44,000 pounds (20,000kg), the 415 isn't a very large aircraft. It is quick and agile, though, and its payload of more than 1,600 gallons (6,000l) of water-foam mixture is quite respectable. Maximum speed is 200 knots, with a rated stall speed of only 68 knots. Power comes from twin Pratt and Whitney (Canada) PW123AF turboprops, each pumping out 2380 hp during takeoff.

Canadair 415s and similar fire-fighting amphibians have some real virtues for a "fire boss." An "alert" fire tanker like the 415 can be airborne five minutes after receiving an assignment and can generally be on-scene in about fifteen minutes. One of the primary missions for this plane is "initial attack"— dropping its 1,600 gallons of Class A foam on a fresh lightning strike, for example, to knock it down before it gets much headway. Depending on how far the aircraft must go to reload, an amphibious fire tanker like the 415 can drop on the fire typically from six to ten times an hour, unloading up to about 16,000 gallons (61,000l) of borate fire-retardant foam on the fire. Like the Mars, the 415 refills its tanks by skimming across a lake or ocean, quickly scooping up another load and returning for another drop.

The aircraft needs an open body of water about 4,000 feet (1,200m) long, most of it for the approach and departure phase of the maneuver; the pilot brings the plane down, maintaining 75 knots indicated airspeed during the scoop, and keeps the plane skimming along for about twelve seconds. Then the scoop doors are closed, power is applied, and it climbs back out.

Back at the fire, the pilot has a very dangerous problem. Fires, particularly in the

An Avid Amphibian, photographed off the coast near Monterey, California. Intended as a kit plane for home construction, the Amphibian is one of only a few aircraft built to this design.

Canadian and American west, begin in little box canyons, or on the sides of steep ridges. If they start with a lightning strike (and they usually do), they tend to do so in the afternoon, when it is hot. Those conditions make the aircraft and its engines less efficient. Smoke makes the target more difficult to see, and makes other aircraft in the area potentially invisible. A good drop should be about 110 feet (35m) above the fire, with the airspeed at about 110 knots. A lot of fire tanker pilots die making these drops.

Canadair 415s give the pilot an extra margin of safety with a strong, stable airframe, very powerful engines, and good visibility. These planes have been used quite extensively, not only across Canada but also in Virginia and North Carolina, the Los Angeles basin, as well as in France.

The de Havilland DHC-2 Beaver

Back in the late 1940s, as wartime economies converted to peaceful requirements, de Havilland designed a small utility plane to

A brightly colored Kit Fox sits on an Idaho lake awaiting passengers.

serve the thousands of miners, foresters, hydroelectric engineers and construction workers, and tourists flocking in droves to the remote backwoods. At the time, prewar and war-surplus aircraft were pretty much all that was available. But operations in the bush are hard on airplanes, with many short hops, high-performance takeoffs, and hard landings on rough strips or choppy lakes. Planes in this kind of service wear out, crash, or simply disappear. It might be hard on pilots, but it makes for a great market for aircraft manufacturers.

De Havilland designed the Beaver to serve the bush pilot market with a compact, agile, powerful high-wing aircraft with superb short-field takeoff and landing characteristics. Phil Garratt was head of de Havilland then, and his vision was of a kind of half-ton pickup truck with wings, designed to go anywhere, and come back again with another load. De Havilland interviewed bush pilots to discover what qualities were important in the new design, and one of the recurrent themes was for a plane with very good short-field performance, the ability to clear the tall trees at the edge of a small lake or short landing strip.

The response was an all-metal plane with thick wings, huge engine, and slotted flaps that could climb out like a rocket. Stressed for the beating that bush planes get, the Beaver was intended to be a robust, muscular machine that could get in and out of any little puddle, and deliver a few cases of dynamite, half a dozen miners, and maybe a few large pieces of a bulldozer when it arrived. The Beaver was an instant hit.

The first Beaver flew in 1947. Only 30 feet (9m) long, it has a 48-foot (14.5m) wingspan and an empty weight of about 2,900 pounds (1,300kg). The Beaver will absorb another 2,200 pounds (1,000kg) of fuel, crew, and payload, and still get airborne. Power for the little aircraft is provided by a 450-hp Pratt and Whitney R-985 AN-14B Wasp Jr. radial

In Alaska, where the population is sparse and the terrain is mountainous, one out of three people owns a seaplane.

engine—a lot of power for a plane of this size. It will carry so much weight that pilots in the Canadian bush routinely strap boats, refrigerators, and similar bulky cargo to the Beaver's floats. Naturally the airplane is not very quick or agile with that kind of load; 100 knots is about all one can expect for cruise, and it will make a steep approach better than a steep climb-out. Without the load, and with-

out floats, a Beaver will perk along at about 130 mph (210kph) at cruise, 160 mph (255kph) when attempting to escape from fighters. With normal load it is supposed to climb at about 1,000 fpm, but since Beavers are normally overloaded, this doesn't happen often. Maximum range is 470 miles (750km).

This performance was noted by the U.S. Army and Air Force during 1951, when the

Beaver won competitions for utility aircraft. Both services bought nearly a thousand Beavers. They served with distinction in Korea and for about fifteen years after. Had a dispute with the Air Force not required the U.S. Army to discard nearly all its fixed-wing aircraft during the 1970s, the Beaver might still be serving.

Although the U.S. Army and Air Force bought up most of the 1,600 Beavers built,

Float planes deliver fishermen and hunters to pristine backwoods streams and lakes, part of the important tourist industry in such regions as Canada, Alaska, and New Zealand.

about 600 went into service in the Canadian bush, and into remote territory in about sixty nations around the world.

The Beaver is now more than fifty years old but is still the mainstay of many floatplane operators around the world. They serve in Canada and Alaska, of course, by the hundreds. But others work in the Caribbean, Australia, and New Zealand, carrying tourists to secluded beach resorts. A few Beavers have been relegated to museums—it is, after all, probably Canada's most successful aircraft design—but most are still at work, carrying too much gear and too many people into spaces that are too small for any other craft.

Seaplanes Into the Sunset

Although not as common or as important as during the early years of aviation, seaplanes and flying boats continue to be a vital part of modern aviation. Thousands of float-equipped Cessnas and de Havilland planes provide transportation throughout the wilderness regions of Canada, Alaska, the Maine backwoods, and the Great Lakes area of the American Midwest. Charter operators fly scuba divers to remote reefs all around the Caribbean, Australia, and the South Pacific. And historic seaplanes are included in displays at the Smithsonian Air and Space

Museum in Washington, D.C., the Martin Museum near Baltimore, Maryland, and many other aviation-oriented sites.

One of the best ways to research information is through the Internet's vast and frequently-changing resources. Some sample sites are listed in the appendix at the back of this book, but there are hundreds of others. If you're interested in learning to fly seaplanes, you'll find dozens of flight schools around the world offering instruction. Numerous museums featuring floatplanes and flying boats are open to the public, too, probably more than a few near you.

108

Cessna dominates the floatplane marketplace worldwide, and with good reason—many thousands of their airframes are available, ready to convert from landplane to seaplane configuration. This one is based in Valdez, Alaska.

A Beaver in the Bush

Canadian bush pilot Kaviv A. Momoh has flown Beavers throughout the Great White North. He shares his thoughts on the plane here.

The Beaver—what's so great about it anyway? Ask anyone who has flown one and you're sure to get a bunch of answers, but here's what I like about it: It has far better takeoff and landing performance than most other floatplanes. It has a big engine (985 cubic inches) and big, fat wings (more than a 48-foot [14.5m] span) and lots of flap. The ailerons also droop together to act as slotted flaps. Even at gross weight, the takeoff run is relatively short, and the climb performance (over obstacles) is great. Only when you tie big things on the side (like snowmobiles, refrigerators, and boats) does the performance get lousy.

The Beaver can carry a lot of weight and bulk, but not so much as to destroy your back by the end of the season. Up to seven people can sit in a Beaver, although five is the usual along with 400 or 500 pounds [180–225kg] of baggage and 35 gallons [133l] of fuel—enough for around an hour and forty-five minutes of flying. If longer flights are the order, there are a total of three fuel tanks in the belly to rely on, and an optional two in the wingtips.

Possibly the only shortcoming that the Beaver has is speed—or rather the lack of it. On floats it cruises at around 100 knots, give or take some. This is nice in a way, though. You can slide the window down on hot days without making it too windy inside. And opening the window doesn't make much difference on the noise level inside either—it's already so loud.

The Beaver that I flew recently—unlike the majority of Beavers—has extra fins on the tail, and lacks a dorsal fin. The reason is to provide improved directional stability because it has larger floats. Having larger floats is handy. The plane rides higher and can get into shallower spots. It does slow the plane down a bit though and creates one nasty little tendency—digging in and starting to nose over on landing if you have a forward center of gravity and aren't careful. But that only happens to you once. It's easy to control after you get the feel of the machine. Speaking about digging in, I once had a passenger in the front seat who rebelliously unfastened the seat belt just before we landed, giving me an evil eye at the same time.

For the most part, there are two kinds of businesses that operate floatplanes in the bush. One is a lodge or "outfitter," which uses a plane to supply its own tourism camps. The other is a "charter operator," which doesn't own any camps and flies for hire instead (like an airline). I found that just doing charters is more fun than having to maintain camps as well. All that you concentrate on is the flying.

I'll give you an idea of what it's like to work for a charter company. When offered a position, I jumped at the chance to work for my present employer, Huron Air. It isn't a large company—four pilots and five commercial aircraft—but it is very busy, efficiently run, and everything is done by the book. This company, like many others of this nature, provides fully equipped housing. This frees you from having to pay rent (although it also keeps you on the base where you are handy). In return for this and a good salary, you are expected to treat the machines as if they were your own, always be professional and courteous, and work your hardest.

Although the company doesn't own any outpost camps, tourism still forms a large portion of the work. A large lodge and three other outfitters are the main customers. They don't have aircraft of their own, so they hire the air service to fly their customers in and out. This makes it easier for everyone; the air service doesn't have to deal with camps, the outfitter doesn't have to deal with the intricacies of running an air service, and the pilots don't have to do anything except airplane-related duties. (We don't have dock hands so we [pilots] still have to load the planes, and the like.)

Our usual days for lodge and outfitter customers are Fridays, Saturdays, and Sundays. We prepare on Thursday evening by lining up drums of fuel (for the lodge) in front of the Otter, and I also load "my" Beaver with about forty cases of beer—drinking beer is a very important part of a fishing vacation. Every evening the front tanks in the Beavers are always filled so we can go at a moment's notice, on the following morning.

At first light we check the weather, pump the floats, and do our walk-arounds. After being loaded with fuel drums and propane, the Otter departs, followed by a Beaver every ten minutes thereafter. Once at the lodge, we quickly unload the goods, reinstall the seats, and take on four passengers (seven or eight in the Otter) and baggage. The time from touchdown to takeoff is usually around eight minutes and the flight takes only twenty-five. We continue doing this until around noon.

After a break, we fly the other outfitter's customers and supplies. It is tiring, but fun (most of the time). Once the flying is done for the day, the planes are refueled, cleaned inside and out, and put to bed.

During the rest of the week, we work for Ontario Hydro, MNR, EC, line-cutters, prospectors, miners, and the forestry industry. We also do a lot of work for the First Nations (native communities). Flying for Ontario Hydro basically involves taking them to one of several dams, and waiting until they have finished their work. While waiting, the walleye and pike fishing is great. The work is always interesting, and one of their common destinations, "Summit Control Dam," is also the trickiest. Numerous whirlpools and eddies form in the strong current. The plane gets gently rocked from side to side by the frothy water as you slowly approach the sluice gates, before turning out into a calmer spot to tie up. Taxiing an expensive plane in this turmoil is a bit nerve-racking and takes getting used to.

After all the math is done, a monthly average of six individual legs each day is flown, although it actually varies between two and fifteen. Most of the legs take between twenty-five minutes and two hours.

The best thing about a float-flying job is that you go to such a wide variety of places, always encountering new or challenging situations. You are rarely faced with an opportunity to get bored.

Alas, work isn't everything. Unfortunately, there is only one channel that we can get on the tube and also only one station on the radio. If any real entertainment is to be had, it is by meeting up with some of the "enemy" pilots. There are several other companies in the area, and although there is competition, pilots always get along great together and have a blast.

This little Cessna has delivered a couple of passengers to the very face of a glacier in Alaska, a common chore for some sight-seeing operators in this vast but sparsely populated state. In areas where spectacular sights are unreachable by regular aircraft, seaplanes are able to bring in the tourists.

Even ultra-lights have been adapted to work off floats. This little amphibian scoots around the South Pacific reefs as part of the Moorings company's yacht fleet.

Republic SeaBees were once common seaplanes and had some real virtues, such as excellent visibility and cabin access, thanks to that pusher prop, plus good payload and flight characteristics.

Above: A Bird Innovator gleams against a deep blue sky.

Opposite: A Beaver takes in the sights newar Princess Louisa Waterfall in British Columbia.

Above: A little Cessna seaplane saddles up to the dock at Misty Fjords National Park in Alaska.

Opposite: A pilot watches the sun go down after a long day of flying his GAF Nomad in the Canadian wilderness.

Resources

Where to Visit and Where to Fly

Forest Industries
Forest Industries in British Columbia, Canada, is the current owner of surviving Martin Mars aircraft. You can reach them at (250) 723-6225, or visit their website at *www.martinmars.com.*

Kenmore Air Seaplanes
For tours throughout the coastal Pacific Northwest, give Kenmore Air a call at (800) 543-9595, or check out their website at *www.kenmoreair.com.*

The Luftwaffe Homepage. Here, find specifications on the German Luftwaffe's seaplane catapult barges during World War II: *http://home4.inet.tele.dk/mholm/catapult.htm.*

San Francisco Seaplane Tours
For one of the best views of the San Francisco Bay Area, book a seaplane tour. For information, call (888) SEAPLANE (1-888-732-7526), or check out their website at *www.seaplane.com.*

The Seaplanes Pilots Association
This organization of civil seaplane pilots offers information on seaplanes history, flight schools, merchandise, and other resources. Contact them at 421 Aviation Way, Frederick, MD 21701, Tel: (301) 695-2083, or visit their website at *www.seaplanes.org.*

Tofino Airlines, Ltd.
Visitors to the Vancouver, British Columbia, area can tour the region by air or fly into the back country to fish or hunt aboard Tofino Air's floatplanes. Contact them at (250) 725-4454, or check out their website at *www.tofino-bc.com/tofinoair.*

The U.S. Naval Historical Center
The history of the U.S. Navy, including seaplanes and flying boats, is well documented by the navy's historical center at the Washington Navy Yard, 805 Kidder Breese SE, Washington, D.C. 20374-5060. Visit their website at *www.history.navy.mil.*

VP Navy This organization maintains a history of naval patrol planes and personnel. Centered in Waldorf, Maryland, you can find them on the web at *www.vpnavy.com.*

Photo Credits

©Gordon Bain: pp. 2,7,50,79,104,105,117
FPG: pp. 31,40
©Hans Halberstadt: pp. 14,15,43,46,54-55,56,57,22
©William B. Folsom: pp. 92,107,108
King Visual Technology: pp. 16,26,34,35,36-37,74
Leo de Whys, Inc. / ©Angelo Cavalli: pp. 4-5
©Howard Levy: pp. 48,66,69,70,82-83,84,85,87,90,91,92,95
MFPG/ ©Pan Am: pp. 44-45
©Frank B. Mormillo: pp. 68,73,76-77,86
©Vlad Norev: pp. 96-97,98,99
©Michael O'Leary: pp. 12-13,17,18,19,24-25,27,32,33,38,42,49, 51,52,53,58,60-61,62,64,65,67,80,81,88-89, 94,114
©Neil Rabinowitz: pp. 1,10-11,102,106,109,111,112,113,115,116
Terry Gwynn-Jones Collection: pp. 8,20-21,39,41,28,29,30

Index

120